# WHY LITERATURE STILL MATTERS:
# BEAUTY AFTER THE APOCALYPSE

BY JASON M. BAXTER

PUBLISHED BY CASSIODORUS PRESS

Published by Cassiodorus Press

PO Box 567

Madison, NC 27025


www.CassiodorusPress.com

Cover illustration by Gabriel Chou

Cover design and layout by Atlee Northmore

First published in 2024 by Cassiodorus Press


ISBN: 978-1-965520-00-0

Printed and bound in the United States of America.

# ACKNOWLEDGMENTS

I'd like to thank my dear Wyoming friends, Glenn and Ginny Arbery. The title of this book is, in part, a tribute to Glenn's book and teaching and commitment to the craft. I also want to express gratitude to the intrepid and entrepreneurial Angelina Stanford, who will be among the regal and magnanimous souls on Dante's Jupiter. I want to thank my cool, techno-savvy friend at Notre Dame, Brett Robinson, who not only issued me the invitation to give the talk that later became Chapter 1, but who also talked over with me almost every other idea in this book. My friends at the Eighth Day Institute in Wichita heard drafts of Chapter 1 and 2, and my students at Benedictine College, the Angelico Fellows, were the first audience for my thoughts on Wilbur and Franny. My wife, Jodi, has lived through this with me and remains my best critic and friend.

But I would like to dedicate this book to my daughters, Pia (the writer) and Evie (my philosopher). How many passages did I inflict on you, girls?

# PREFACE

## THE STORY OF TWO ISLANDS

This book is about why literature still matters. To get at that, though, I thought I also had to take up two other questions. First, what does literature feel like? If we answer that, we'll be able to say why it's important. The second question is: why has it become so difficult for us to read (or see or listen) with depth, especially poems or paintings or works of music created before the modern world? With Lewis, I'll date "the modern world" to some point in the second half of the nineteenth century, although it was a long time in coming, as I explain below.

Throughout this book, I will frequently compare literature to painting and architecture and music. I want to know what literature would sound like if it were melted down and turned into music, or what literature would look like if it crystallized and became the visual arts.[1] But the fuller answer of why literature still matters is that reading literature feels similar to being immersed in a landscape. Literature, like landscape, has a tactile, palpable, haptic, sensuous dimension. I had encountered this *idea* in Lewis many years before, but I hadn't understood what he was trying to get at until I had two *experiences*

---

1   To help my readers, I've developed a set of my hyperlinked footnotes, which readers can find at my Substack, *Beauty Matters*. And for help finding *that*, readers can go to my website, JasonMBaxter.com.

of my own, experiences of two very different landscapes on two very different islands: Sardinia and Iceland. I narrate my travel experiences of these places in this book as a way of getting at my deeper concern: what does an experience of beauty feel like? What is it good for? How does literature, and her sister arts, attempt to hold onto that beauty? And is it possible that, as our ability to see our landscapes disappears, we are also losing access to our words?

The chapter on Sardinia is upbeat and hopeful. The chapter on Iceland, perhaps appropriately, is cold and a little apocalyptic, but I wanted to explore how deep the problem goes, in order to create a sense of urgency for our project.

# CHAPTER 1

## APOCALYPSE OF THE IMAGINATION: HOW TO BECOME A HUMAN EMOJI

A couple of years ago, I started reading, with my college students, the open letter that Mark Zuckerberg and Priscilla Chan addressed to their infant daughter in 2015. In that letter, the couple made the dazzling claim that they had plans, over the course of their lives, to give away 99% of their Facebook shares to combat disease and inequality. If they really do this, they will become the greatest philanthropists in human history. And so it has always been a little puzzling to me that the letter invokes such a tepid, guarded response from my students when I read it aloud to them in class. They *know* that Zuckerberg and Chan are saying "The Right Things," but for some reason they don't feel moved by what they hear.

Why is that?

The reality is that the letter is so full of hackneyed parental sentiments that it's hard to find anything concrete to disagree with:

Dear Max,

> Your mother and I don't yet have the words to describe the hope you give us for the future. Your new life is full of promise, and we hope you will be happy and healthy so you can explore it fully. You've already given us a reason to reflect on the world we hope you live in. Like all parents, we want you to grow up in a world better than ours today.[1]

So far, so good. Right? And yet despite the recognizable sentiments, my students feel—even if they can't always articulate it—that the letter has a funny tone. There's something off.

Surely, this is partly because the letter gets a little preachy in places: "Right now, we don't always collectively direct our resources at the biggest opportunities and problems your generation will face," they patiently explain to their infant daughter. "Consider disease," they continue: "Today we spend about 50 times more as a society treating people who are sick than we invest in research so you won't get sick in the first place." But nevertheless the Chan Zuckerberg Initiative intends to dedicate itself to "do its part," they say with great originality. Throughout the letter, Zuckerberg is sober but optimistic: "Health is improving. Poverty is shrinking. Knowledge is growing. People are connecting." And what must we do to continue these trends? Get everyone hooked up to the internet, because the "only way to achieve our full potential is to channel the talents, ideas and contributions of every person in the world, because most progress comes from productivity gains through innovation." Given the "technological progress in every field," Zuckerberg hopes that life will soon be "dramatically better than [it is] today." In fact, for him, the great question

---

[1]    All quotations from this letter come from https://chanzuckerberg.com/about/letter-to-max.

is how far we can push "the boundaries on how great a human life can be." Zuckerberg

muses: "Can you learn and experience 100 times more than we do today?" The letter

concludes: "Max, we love you and feel a great responsibility to leave the world a better

place for you and all children. We wish you a life filled with the same love, hope and joy

you give us. We can't wait to see what you bring to this world."

Does it feel like something is missing?

If you're like me, after reading that question a chill runs down your spine, because

it *does* feel like something is missing, but it's difficult to put your finger on what that is.

We've forgotten something, but we can't remember what that was. We need help and

perspective, a perspective we gain by comparing Zuckerberg to the past.

---

Contrasting Zuckerberg's open letter with the poem "A Prayer for My Daughter"

by W. B. Yeats helps us begin to put into words that eerie absence we feel but have trouble

speaking.[2] Unlike the easy-going positivity of Zuckerberg, Yeats experiences the troubled

doubts of a father who has brought an innocent child into a deceptive, manipulative, and

apocalyptically evil world. Using lines that echo his terrifying "Second Coming," Yeats

pictures himself pacing back and forth while a storm rages outside and his child sleeps:

> Once more the storm is howling…
>
> And for an hour I have walked and prayed
>
> Because of the great gloom that is in my mind.
>
> I have walked and prayed for this young child an hour
>
> And heard the sea-wind scream up the tower…

---

2    As mentioned in the preface, I've created a set of hyperlinked footnotes to all of the music, paintings, and architecture

mentioned throughout this book. Those can be found on my Substack, *Beauty Matters*.

> Imagining in excited reverie
>
> That the future years had come,
>
> Dancing to a frenzied drum,
>
> Out of the murderous innocence of the sea.[3]

Yet in the midst of this soul-sickness, or perhaps, because of it, Yeats reaches down within and stirs up the embers of his heart and finds the capacity to pray:

> May she be granted beauty and yet not
>
> Beauty to make a stranger's eye distraught
>
> Or hers before a looking glass, for such,
>
> Being made beautiful overmuch,
>
> Consider beauty a sufficient end,
>
> Lose natural kindness and maybe
>
> The heart revealing intimacy
>
> That chooses right, and never find a friend.[4]

In other words, Yeats prays for beauty, but it is not like the beauty of Helen, who became ensnared in her own appearance and felt the pressure to live her whole life on the periphery of her skin, acting in accordance with the weight of other people's expectations. Yeats instead adds something about his daughter's heart:

---

3    W. B. Yeats, "A Prayer for My Daughter," Academy of American Poets, accessed November 15, 2024, https://poets.org/poem/prayer-my-daughter. I am quoting lines 1, 7–10, 13–16.

4    Yeats, v. 17–24.

> May she become a flourishing hidden tree
>
> That all her thoughts may like the linnet be,
>
> And have no business but dispensing round
>
> Their magnanimities of sound.[5]

In other words, Yeats prays for her heart and mind to be full of joyous thoughts, for her interior life to be rich with insights and the love of fugitive moments of beauty. The Irish poet gets at all this with the curious metaphor of a tree full of linnets. Then he further prays that her heart may never be "choked with hate," and he utters his hopes that, once she has driven all hatred from her heart, her soul will "recover radical innocence, and learn at last that it is self-delight, self-appeasing, self-affrighting, and that its own sweet will is Heaven's will." That is to say, if a soul is not at rest with itself—if it is not clean—it will never find contentment, no matter how many resources it has access to. And so, Yeats doesn't just admit that "your mother and I don't yet have the words to describe the hope you give us for the future," but rather forces his mind to restlessly range over the worlds of myth, nature, and craft in search of likenesses: storms, winds, towers, oceans, and trees with delicate birds chirping within.

Clearly, the way of Yeats is not scientific, but neither is it naive or primitive, which is what we, living in this technological age, often reflexively think of when we hear *unscientific*. Yeats, and the long tradition within which he stands, does not primarily see the natural world as a set of resources which need to be mined, analyzed, pulled to pieces, and rebuilt into more useful things like plastic and microwaves. Rather, the natural world's chief value is found when it is "looked upon," loved, internalized, and then re-spoken, or painted or played or prayed. We'll have more to say about this soon, but for now take a

---

5    Yeats, v. 41–44.

second poem by Yeats as an illustration, "The Lake Isle of Innisfree":

> I will arise and go now, and go to Innisfree,
>
> And a small cabin build there, of clay and wattles made;
>
> Nine bean-rows will I have there, a hive for the honey-bee,
>
> And live alone in the bee-loud glade.
>
> And I shall have some peace there, for peace comes dropping slow,
>
> Dropping from the veils of the morning to where the cricket sings;
>
> There midnight's all a glimmer, and noon a purple glow,
>
> And evening full of the linnet's wings.
>
> I will arise and go now, for always night and day
>
> I hear lake water lapping with low sounds by the shore;
>
> While I stand on the roadway, or on the pavements grey,
>
> I hear it in the deep heart's core.[6]

You can tell that Yeats is already one of us, a man of bustle and haste and modern anxiety who finds himself too often on roadways and gray pavement. And yet, "in the deep heart's core," he hears an alluring call to peace and depth, which sounds to him like the quiet "lake water lapping." And so, reaching down into that secret part of the heart, he lays hold of this longing for a life of simplicity and unshowy harmony. For Yeats, an island in the middle of a fresh-water lake in northern Ireland, Innisfree—with its "bee-loud

---

[6]    W. B. Yeats, "The Lake Isle of Innisfree," Poetry Foundation, accessed November 15, 2024, https://www.poetryfounda-tion.org/poems/43281/the-lake-isle-of-innisfree. I here quote the poem in full.

glade" and its singing crickets and its midnights "all a glimmer" and its noons with their "purple glow" and the evenings which are "full of the linnet's wings"—is the symbol of this dwelling in communion with nature and being at peace with himself. Peace is difficult to come by, though. We know that. And if it does come, it only comes "dropping slow," in part because finding peace means becoming peaceful. It means writing simplicity into your nerves and ways of being. And so, Yeats will need to practice at peacefulness. He'll need to be content with "a small cabin" made of "clay and wattle," and he will need to tend his "nine bean-rows."

The point is this: Yeats uses the island of Innisfree as a kind of laboratory, a thought experiment. In his mind, he builds a life on this island, and then frames it out in the musical cadences of poetic meter and in the poetic harmonies of rhyme. And then he makes it all sticky and memorable by using techniques of doubling back (*anadiplosis*: "I will arise and go now, and go to Innisfree…") and inversions of ordinary syntax to slow us down ("and a small cabin build there…"). He fills his poem with natural sounds ("lake water lapping"), sensuous memorable coinages ("bee-loud glade"), unexpectedly concrete details ("of clay and wattles made"), but also fluttering motions whose vibrations we can feel as they whizz past us ("evening full of linnet's wings"). We *feel* weather, seasons, and the heat and humidity of noon. We hear water and bees and feel the vibrations of birds somewhere close but out of sight. We feel the dirt of the bean rows and the simple solidity of made objects. In this way, Yeats doesn't just say he wants peace; he works it out in his mind, tills the soil of language, so that he can touch peace and hear it and hold it. In a way, the lines of his poem are like the rows of plants in a garden, with so much life and motion and atmosphere between them.

This second poem also puts us in a position to appreciate what is special about Yeats's "A Prayer for My Daughter" because, in *that* poem, Yeats does not content himself with a single set of images for peace (a garden or a tree with birds), nor only with images for strength (towers and storms). Rather, the Irish poet, with one foot in antiquity and one foot on the gray pavement of modernity, knows that the soul is as deep as the world is wide, and, like a Liszt of words, he will need all the keys on the keyboard to reach it (I was listening to Liszt's "Les jeux d'eaux a la Villa d'Este" while writing this). Yeats will need the bass notes, because there are deep parts of the soul, but also the highest treble notes, in which we long for goods we hardly have words for. Or, if you prefer, you could say Yeats needed every instrument in the orchestra. If the world is a book of symbols, Yeats wanted every page of it, because the soul is deep and wide and complicated, and we need the whole world to think and feel through it.

This, at any rate, is the artistic and literary tradition that Yeats stood within, one which Pierre Hadot called the "Orphic" Tradition, named after the legendary poet in ancient mythology Orpheus, whose poetry could penetrate trees and make them sway.[7] By his music, Orpheus could calm the hearts of savage beasts and lay a hushing spell on the underworld so that, once, even hell rested from its meaningless toil to listen for a while. According to this tradition, man and world were made for one another. We belong to it, as much as it belongs to us. The natural world is a great book of "symbols," that is, natural phenomena that— somehow, someway— resonate and awaken some inner part within us. When we look at the moon over the sea— or a waterfall or cliff or skylark or nightingale— we sense a corresponding quality within. The world is like a tuning fork which, brought near to a second tuning fork— in this case, our hearts— causes the latter to vibrate as well. Inspired by what we see, we reach down into that inner depth, and, if we are able, pull out words or images or chords and scales for what we find, words or pictures or sounds we did not previously know we had. In this way, the natural symbol draws out

---

7    See Pierre Hadot's *The Veil of Isis* for more on this tradition.

something that had been "deeper down" and hidden within. And this is why, when you look at a truly great painting, even of some very ordinary landscape, like Constable's painting of Salisbury, you have an incredible experience: on the one hand, it all seems so plain and quotidian, but, at the same time, it seems saturated with a quality that makes it realer, denser, and slower than anything that could show up in ordinary life. The poet Samuel Taylor Coleridge once described the experience he had, one melancholic evening, when he looked up at a huge moon hanging over the sea at night. He later wrote in his diary:

> In looking at objects of Nature while I am thinking, as at yonder moon dim-glimmering thro' the dewy window-pane, I seem rather to be seeking, as it were *asking* for, a symbolical language for something within me that already and forever exists, than observing anything new. Even when that latter is the case, yet still I have always an obscure feeling as if that new phenomena were the dim awaking of a forgotten or hidden Truth of my inner Nature.[8]

In addition to paintings and poems, there are also works of music, like Ralph Vaughn Williams's "Lark Ascending" or Mendelssohn's overture *The Hebrides*. In the latter, Mendelssohn begins with an anxious melodic motif that repeats itself, like the swirling of dangerous waters off the coast of Scotland. But this melodic motif, though repeated, goes through every possible variation, sometimes in different instrumentations (now horns, now woodwinds, now strings), sometimes in new keys, sometimes in rising crescendos that later

---

8   Samuel Taylor Coleridge, *Anima Poetae: from the Unpublished Notebooks*, ed. Ernest Hartley Coleridge (London: William Heinemann, 1895), 136.

fade away into hushed decrescendos. But, at the same time, this repeated melody is laid on top of other patterns. The strings sometimes rise slowly and steadily, note by note, over several bars, representing the swell of great masses of water, which, of course, culminates in a clash of cymbals, representing the iridescent mist of a million drops of spray. You could say that Mendelssohn did for music what Yeats did for words and Constable did for paint. He aimed to create an art that got at the complexity and range of the natural world, but in a way that whispered to some deeper quality of soul.

We are now ready to come back to our point of departure, because we can now explain why Zuckerberg's letter feels so eerie and why we feel that something is weirdly absent: Zuckerberg's imaginative vocabulary is suffocatingly limited. Yeats needed the whole book of the world—with its stars and seasons and trees and birds and winds and storms, towers, myths, beauties, wars, and beasts—to sound the soul, discover its range and depth, and *then* pray for a life of fullness for his daughter. But when we hear Zuckerberg speak of his plans (not prayers, mind you) for his daughter's wellbeing, we find him, not surprisingly, using metaphors drawn from the practical application of mathematical functions, sketched out in order to find vertex coordinates—that is, those graphable points that represent maxima and minima for market opportunities. Most chillingly, anytime that Zuckerberg does address Max herself—rather than turning the birth of his infant daughter into a press release for his new foundation—we find him contemplating her productivity value over time, or enumerating the resources he intends to assemble to make her generation's output 100 times more than his. Max's life is a graph, whose function has been vertically stretched; given that the domain of inputs at her disposal will approach the unlimited, the range of her work outputs will grow exponentially. And as Byung-Chul Han bleakly puts it, this is one of the chief characteristics of our time: "The nineteenth century discovered work, and play became increasingly distrusted. There was now much more work than play: the world resembled a factory rather than a theater."[9] The whole world of work "appropriates the person himself and turns him into a highly efficient site of production. The whole person is incorporated into the production process."[10]

But there are no subjunctives; no tender wishes; no prayers for quiet intimacy; nothing about ceremony, grace, inwardness, friendship, or even fulfillment.

Max, I imagine, will be very productive.

Do you think she will be happy?

---

The Charlie Chaplin film *Modern Times* deals humorously with the real anxieties surrounding the modern imperative to become "highly efficient site[s] of production."[11] Chaplin's character, of course, is a total failure at conforming to the new world of mechanization: he likes his leisurely lunch breaks and he can't keep up with the widget-lines that need their doo-hickies tightened. At one point, he gets pulled into the machine and swished around like laundry in a washer. It's very funny. But you can feel the anxiety underneath the humor: what if our lives ever became the mere gears and axles of a machine's function?

The film ends on an upbeat note, though, because at the time of its release there was yet one area which was resistant to such attempts at flattening, graphing, and reverse engineering: the interior domain of the human psyche, which included love, subjectivity, dreams, and hopes. My subjectivity—what I loved, who I fell in love with, what I thought, how I felt—was still *mine*, even if the space in which my body operated and the time during which I worked now largely belonged to the grid. At least I held the real me, safe

---

9    Byung-Chul Han, *Saving Beauty*, trans. David Steuer (Cambridge: Polity Press, 2018), 19.

10   Han, 18.

11   Han, 18.

within.

Enter modern marketing and propaganda.

And Mark Zuckerberg.

In particular, Zuckerberg's genius was that he created a grid—a virtual space— in which all day, every day, you and I, and billions of other people, gleefully translate our own emotions into coordinate points of desire. I mean, of course, that by participating in social media, pioneered by corporations like Facebook, we've crowdsourced market research.

Imagine the following scenario: you go onto YouTube and listen to a song, say, Rihanna's "This Is What You Came For," and "like" it. You see a pair of shoes and save them to a wish list. You are providing coordinate points which relate aesthetic experience with a product. Sometimes you add a comment: "this song was SO beautiful" or "this song made me cry." What if I also had access to your email account and text messages, such that I could run a search and determine under what circumstances you send emails in which you use such phrases of emotion? And if I could then correlate that with the websites you visit, and how long you stay, how long you linger over that picture, and how much your pupils dilate while doing so? Whom do you call, and for how long? How frequently do you text? And then you have enabled location recognition on almost every app you use, so I also know where you are and where you go shortly after saying or wishing for such things or texting this emoji to that person. I can thus correlate the time of day with the time of year and create a vast network of emotional connections for you, and how they play out within your world of products and relationships, thereby creating for you a unique word cloud of impressions which is your individualized emotional DNA, your own online data-print. This is the world of predictive, big data capitalism that Shoshana

Zuboff and Anton Barba-Kay have described in detail.[12]

For our present purposes, I am less interested in the political and sociological questions involved in surveillance capitalism's "datafication" of the universe and am more interested in the psychological question of what happens to me if I get into the habit of this lifestyle datafication. And I am interested in *that* because, as someone who has dedicated his life to teaching the "Great Books" to students, I'm interested in how, or if, they are absorbing them. What would happen, for instance, if my face-to-face relationship with you began to feel like a subset of my virtual interactions with you? In other words, if all day, every day, when you send me a text which amuses me and I "like" it, and then I send something back to you and you "love" it, is it possible that when I am in front of you and you say something I agree with, that how I respond to you could begin to feel like an imperfect attempt to "like" what you're saying, with slam effect? What I really need you to do is text that to me to be "real" so I can express my "like" properly. Otherwise, my assent does not feel complete.

Similarly, if I am in the habit of consuming information and news on Facebook, where I am allowed a restricted set of six reactions (like, love, wow, angry, sad, and haha), could it happen that, over time, my mind and heart would cease feeling anything more than these primitive motions of affirmation and disaffirmation, in which adverbs of quality and qualification disappear? Of the vast range of difficult, evasive, and fugitive spiritual impulses, could we be voluntarily cooperating in the simplification of our interior lives, and, by doing so, begin to lose the ability to feel the need for anything greater? I like something, I love something; or I hate something, or I totally hate something. Our emotions unfold on a one-dimensional number line, their strength measured by the distance

---

12   See Zuboff's *The Age of Surveillance: The Fight for a Human Future at the New Frontier of Power* and Barba-Kay's *A Web of Our Own Making: The Nature of Digital Formation.*

from the origin. As David Auerbach puts it:

> If [the restriction of the responses] has the effect of narrowing emo-
> tional diversity, social media and advertising companies view this
> tradeoff as the necessary cost of gathering better data on users. The
> restricted emotional language employed by Facebook is a language a
> computer can understand and manipulate at scale. The simplified lan-
> guage of a core set of emotional reactions bridges the computation-
> al-human gap.[13]

Perhaps it is not surprising, then, that some researchers estimate that the daily
active vocabulary of teenagers is down to 800 words a day. And although it might not be
the case that our vocabularies are *smaller* than those of our grandparents' grandparents
(they might have said "lurid" and "tantalizing," but we have words they did not, like
"bandwidth" and "to network"), we certainly use a *narrower* vocabulary, a smaller domain
for the words that make up our mental machinery. As Kristen Page points out in her book
*The Wonders of Creation*, there is a phenomenon sociologists call "plant blindness": "the
inability to recognize or notice plants in our environment, or the inability to recognize
the importance of plants and plant biodiversity." Page laments that "the campaigns
to increase children's literacy regarding plants and the environment seem to be falling
short." She continues:

> In 2007 the *Oxford Junior Dictionary* removed close to forty words relating
> to the natural world in order to make space for words describing our

---

13   See David Auerbach's "How Facebook Has Flattened Human Communication."

more solitary and digital world. Words like *acorn*, *wren*, *bramble*, *dandelion*, and *willow* were removed to make way for words such as *blog*, *broadband*, *chatroom*, and *MP3*.[14]

In other words, the rich language we've inherited—made up of metaphors, adjectives, adverbs, qualified statements, unusual utterances, literary allusions to well-loved characters, and phrases that are memorable because of their rhythm or rhetorical effects—is being flattened into a primitive set of objects and attributes, with slam effect. If I am right, by voluntarily habituating ourselves to translating our desires into graphable space, we are making the translation process ever easier, because the gap between our original emotions and the fabricated responses is psychologically closing.

Can you turn yourself into a human emoji?

I was writing this very part of the book on an airplane and wondering about that question, when I had to put away my computer to land. After we landed, the carrier put on some upbeat music, presumably to help put us passengers in a good mood while we waited to deplane. The song they played was "Sunshine" by OneRepublic. It's a catchy song, an upbeat celebration of how accelerating patterns of consumption can help you feel good, as well as an almost perfect reduction of all of human life to a giant thumbs-up emoji:

> Running through this strange life
> Chasin' all them green lights
> Throwin' off the shade

14  Kristen Page, *The Wonders of Creation: Learning Stewardship from Narnia and Middle Earth* (Lisle, Illinois: IVP Academic, 2022), ch. 1.

> For a little bit of sunshine
>
> Hit me with them good vibes
>
> Pictures on my phone like
>
> Everything is so fire

Throughout the song, the lyrics not only associate speed ("running," "chasin'") with happiness ("sunshine," "good vibes"), but they also imply that we gain access to these things by means of our technological tools ("pictures on my phone"), a connection reenforced by the music video. Not only are the band members portrayed as emotionally infantile, exaggerated, animated versions of themselves—like Scooby Doo characters—but they are shown feverishly chasing all those "good vibes": lifting weights, riding roller coasters, racing through airports, flying around the world, surfing, holding concerts on the beach, and going for bicycle rides. But all of these experiences are mediated through technological devices. While blazing through tourist spots in Europe on a scooter, they take pictures and videos on their smart phones of sites they only have seconds to see. While boxing, they wear VR glasses. They play music before fans who record them, smart watches glow and send them notifications that it's time to go on tour, and we even watch them watching themselves on their phones. As the lyrics put it: "I don't know any other way to say this / Can't slow down trying to keep up with the changes." What's more, all of these scenes unfold in a manic montage of jump cuts, in which fictive shots or scene changes occur more than one time per second. One of the verses sums it all up:

> I've been working on my tunnel vision
>
> Trynna get a new prescription
>
> Taking swings and even missing

But I don't care

I'm dancing more, just a little bit

Breathing more, just a little bit

Care a little less, just a little bit

Like life is woo hoo!

I'm making more, just a little bit

Spend a little more to get rid of it

It's difficult to think of a song that is closer to the Platonic form of pure marketing—a huge, generic "thumbs up" vibe—which does not sell any product in particular but promotes, in general, a life of consumption: purchase, move, seek, fly, run, buy. The faster you do this, the more good vibes you'll consume. But you'll need devices to augment your productivity and tools to amplify your power, otherwise, you won't be able to "learn and experience 100 times more than we do today." No wonder American Express pays for one of the ads you have to watch before the video begins!

But, again, if we, like the characters we watch, spend our hours and minutes and seconds uploading our emotions into the system so that we download the energy into our lives and, by means of our devices, become high-octane, animated versions of ourselves, will we also slowly lose access to the emotional subtlety found in the rich treasury of our inherited language? It helps to compare the amped up vision of life in "Sunshine" with a passage from Thomas Hardy's ineffably beautiful *Far from the Madding Crowd*. At a certain point, the heroine, Bathsheba Everdeen, goes for an evening walk, hoping to avoid the lover she has just jilted. Here is Hardy's description of Bathsheba's wandering in nature:

She went out of the house just at the close of a timely thunder-shower, which had refined the air, and daintily bathed the coat of the land, though all beneath was dry as ever. Freshness was exhaled in an essence from the varied contours of bank and hollow, as if the earth breathed maiden breath; and the pleased birds were hymning to the scene. Before her, among the clouds, there was a contrast in the shape of lairs of fierce light which showed themselves in the neighbourhood of a hidden sun, lingering....[15]

Unfortunately, Bathsheba does run into Farmer Boldwood, who has this telling response to his cruel beloved:

He came on looking upon the ground, and did not see Bathsheba till they were less than a stone's throw apart. He looked up at the sound of her pit-pat, and his changed appearance sufficiently denoted to her the depth and strength of the feelings paralyzed by her letter. "Oh; is it you, Mr. Boldwood?" she faltered, a guilty warmth pulsing in her face. Those who have the power of reproaching in silence may find it a means more effective than words. There are accents in the eye which are not on the tongue, and more tales come from pale lips than can enter an ear. It is both the grandeur and the pain of the remoter moods that they avoid the pathway of sound. Boldwood's look was unanswerable.[16]

Hardy needs the background of the "freshness" of the evening, which is "exhaling

---

15   Thomas Hardy, *Far From the Madding Crowd* (New York: Harper and Brothers, 1918), 228.

16   Hardy, 229.

maiden breath," to make us attentive to that fugitive emotion which is beneath or beyond

the mere physical appearance: "Boldwood's look [is] unanswerable." To graph such a raw,

fugitive, profound, evasive experience into a "like" or "wow" or "surprise face emoji" or

even a comment ("AWKward!") would be violence.

But the most brilliant feature of Zuckerberg's meta-world is this: once we have

packaged our experiences in digital shrink-wrap—the pictures of the kids on the iPhone,

the little nibbled designer cookie at the boho coffee shop downtown, the selfie of me at

the game— we then post them, so that others can consume our personal life, our manu-

factured feelings, as entertainment. We get likes, our followers consume bits of emotion,

platform makers get data, and our favorite brands purchase our interiority so they can

inseminate their products into our imaginations by means of the people we are following.

So, as I'm going through my feeds, looking for YouTube videos on how to do my nails, I

will, of course, find that dress or pair of shoes and buy them, and, after putting them on,

I'll take new pictures to put images of my upgraded self back online and get even more

likes. It's a virtuous cycle in which what I download into my life helps me upgrade my

social value in the virtual currency of likes. I sell my enhanced image in the market place

of "wows." Everyone's happy!

Mark Zuckerberg must be so proud of us!

I bet he hardly has the words to describe the hope we give him for the future.

———————————————

We said earlier that the "sticky" poetry of Yeats, if translated into music, would

sound like Mendelssohn. Zuckerberg's vision of the world might be better translated by

the music of John Adams.

In particular, I have in mind Adams's 1986, four-minute *Short Ride in a Fast Machine*,

especially as interpreted by the animation of Victor Craven. In contrast to Mendelssohn's layered musical texture, Adams simplifies his composition. Each part of the orchestra plays a looping melodic cell made up of only two, three, or four notes, as if various parts of the orchestra made up a series of interlocking gears and wheels and axles in a machine. Over the course of the piece, all of those instruments speed up a lot, and then we hear knocking and ringing and clanging and booming from the percussion section. In other words, Adams engineered his orchestra; it's a great machine that lurches forward, jerkily at first, but gains momentum and efficiency with each couple of measures. In the overture to his opera *Doctor Atomic*, which retold Oppenheimer's spiritual struggle with the bomb long before Nolan did, Adams literally uses machine noises of accelerating turbines and the buzz of electrical circuitry. Music made by robots for robots.

But if Zuckerberg's approach to life is less "philosophical" than popular—if it's more of a "life hack" than a system of thought—then it's probably more appropriate to liken Zuckerberg's pop philosophy to pop music, such as Calvin Harris and Rihanna's "This Is What You Came For" in C Major, with a tempo of 124 beats a minute. It now has close to 2.8 billion views on YouTube, although, admittedly, 117 of those were mine. The exact same melody is repeated six times, one time an octave higher, and sometimes with different electronic instrumentation. There is one modulation to a new key, but only 40 different words are used throughout the whole song, with particular emphasis on "you" and "oh oh." As one user on YouTube commented: "I heard the word 'you' used, like, 52 times in this song. Anyone else?" Furthermore, Rihanna's voice was engineered to take on a more machine-like sound. One music critic reviewed the song this way: "[it] will definitely be a hit; however, by manipulating her voice so much he's stripped away the personality that made [Rihanna] so compelling. The result is surprisingly soulless."[17]

---

17   Larry Bartleet, "Track Review: Calvin Harris & Rihanna's 'This Is What You Came For' Is No 'We Found Love,'" *NME*

Blogs, April 29, 2016, https://www.nme.com/blogs/nme-blogs/calvin-harris-rihannas-this-is-what-you-came-for-track-re-

Furthermore, the music video is staged inside a vast electronic cube which projects lights, and, at one point, a grid. Rihanna's performance literally takes place within graphable space.

Like "Sunshine," it is a catchy song. But at the same time, the domain of the possible sound has been mechanically limited, radically narrowed to standardized, engineered kilobytes of noise. Almost all complexity has been smoothed out. It's pure pulse. Or, as one listener put it: "0% Bad words / 0% Violence / 0% Racism / 100% yOuuuuYouuuuUu."

"100% you." And *that* comment is a perfect summary of what the Korean-born, German-speaking philosopher Byung-Chul Han has called, in his book *Saving Beauty*, our culture of "excessive positivity," by which he means a world in which we prefer the "smooth" to the beautiful. The beautiful is difficult but the smooth is infinitely agreeable, offering no resistance to never-ending "likability." Indeed, Han goes so far as to call us the practitioners of the "religion of the smooth... a religion of consumption."[18] We surround ourselves with the smooth, taking our new iPhones out of their boxes while holding our breath and running our fingers over their smooth surfaces. Major cities commission the giant, smooth, reflective sculptures of Jeff Koons, the sculptor who boasts that he creates art that no one can disagree with. We love the smooth, Han suggests, because we are in love with the frictionless, accelerating unfolding of infinite positivity: "Why do we today find what is smooth beautiful? Beyond its aesthetic effect, it reflects a general social imperative. It embodies today's *society of positivity.* What is smooth does not *injure.* Nor does it offer any resistance. It is looking for *Like.* The smooth object deletes its *Against.*

18   Han, *Saving Beauty*, 1, 10.

Any form of negativity is removed."[19] The smooth creates "an agreeable feeling" which is easy to consume because it is not weighed down "with any meaning or profound sense. It exhausts itself in a 'Wow.'"[20] And so, for Han, the outward, resistance-less, smooth, and agreeable surfaces we surround ourselves with are the external symbols for what we inwardly long for: "the smooth touchscreen…is a place of de-mystification and total consumption. It produces what one *likes*…. There is no inwardness hidden behind its smooth surface…you only encounter yourself…."[21] We want our phones, our social interactions, our browsing, our shopping, our likes, our music, our sculptures, our open-plan homes, our suburban neighborhoods, the parking lots for our strip centers, and our highways to present no difficulty. But such ease comes at a cost, because smooth things also possess no harmony, no tradition, no history, no ritual, and no inwardness. It's all on the surface: pretty and reflecting me. "100% you."

Jeff Koons is what Zuckerberg's philosophy of life looks like in sculptural form. "Sunshine" or "This Is What You Came For" is what it sounds like in music.

For Han, the cost of our pursuit of infinite positivity and the "aesthetic of the smooth" is the loss of beauty: "the beautiful itself is smoothened out by taking any negativity, any form of shock or injury, out of it. The beautiful is exhausted in a *Like-it.* Aestheticization turns out to be anaesthetization; it sedates our perception…." Based on all this, Han draws the devastating conclusion: "today, the *experience* of beauty is impossible."[22]

---

19   Han, 1.

20   Han, 3.

21   Han, 5.

22   Han, 6–7.

I began this chapter, "Apocalypse of the Imagination," by wondering why Zuckerberg's letter, although full of the "correct," even if hackneyed, parental sentiments, had an eerie feeling of emptiness. We now have Han's explanation: Zuckerberg's vision of the world is "anaesthetizing" and "sedative" because it has eliminated all complexity and all resistance.

What interests me, though, even more than the fact that Zuckerberg writes of his daughter's life as a function that can be vertically stretched, is that he doesn't seem to notice it. Indeed, he doesn't seem to be capable of imagining an alternative.

But what is the alternative?

Before we turn to consider Han's ominous claim that for us "the *experience* of beauty is impossible," I'd like to back up and ask first: what *was* the experience of beauty, anyway? We'll then be in a position to ask what happened to it.

# CHAPTER 2

## HOW TO DIE IN SARDINIA:
## C. S. LEWIS AND THE LANDSCAPE OF LITERATURE

In the northwestern part of the island of Sardinia, there's a small, very Mediterranean town called Alghero, a town the locals call "Barcelonetta," or "baby Barcelona," in part because it has a medieval Gothic downtown, like Barcelona, and in part because it has the largest group of speakers of Catalan outside of Catalonia. But the glory of Sardinia, as everyone knows, is the coast. And so, one day, when I was living there with my family, I got up early in the morning and took a taxi from Alghero up to a long cape, which is, by Italian standards, remote and wild. It was once a medieval hunting preserve for the Catalan rulers but is now a small, undeveloped natural preserve on a peninsula. As soon as I arrived, I walked down a well-kept quarter-mile trail to an old Catalan watch tower.[1] Easy. The morning was cool, the views were perfect, and it was still before 8 a.m. The walk had been short, and I had three large bottles of water, so I thought I would venture on, get farther away, strike out on my own, go farther up. After studying my map for a few minutes, my eyes landed on "Cala d'Inferno" ("The Bay of Hell"). Come on! What Dante scholar wouldn't want to see *that*? It looked like I would have to climb a small

1    I have my original photography of Sardinia available on my Substack: *Beauty Matters.*

mountain, but, once on top of the ridge, I would be able to see the bay. And so, I had a plan: I'd take a jaunty walk up the trail to the top of the hill, see the bay, turn around, come back down to a little town in the valley, find a bus, and be home by lunch. The trails had been so easy and well-groomed so far. Why not *fare lo trekking*, as the Italians say?

I began my walk just as the Mediterranean sun began to heat up. The magical color of sky and water in the Mediterranean is due in part to the so-called Sirocco, the northern wind, which originates over the dry African Sahara, where, growing in heat, it then comes as a blast of dry, hot wind, like air escaping from an oven. As it blows across the Mediterranean, it burns off all its moisture, which accounts for that famous dazzling azure of the summer sky. But as I walked cross country, I also discovered the botanical side-effect of what this dry air means for the plant life in the region. From a distance, Mediterranean landscapes look enchanting and soft. But we're often thinking of the cultivated regions: olives, grape vines, and fig trees. The reality is that *culture* in this climate is fragile, and just a few miles from civilization—as Odysseus so well knew—you can discover what the region would be like without the laborious efforts of tending over millennia. In particular, Sardinia was heavily forested during the unification of Italy, so what we have now are low, squat plants covered in a waxy varnish with serrated edges on their leaves or thorns on their branches, all with the intent to seal in their precious moisture. To my surprise, I discovered that in this shadeless land these squat plants are very tenacious, stiff, resilient, and unforgiving. After all, they can't let people tear off their succulent limbs with impunity. So they venomously guard their life-force by ripping into *you!* Ok. Major mistake one: I was wearing shorts. I should have been wearing heavy gators. But who, after looking at tourist photos from Google, would have been prepared for that? And so, as I hiked along, I was getting pricked and cut every hundred yards or so. Oh, well. It would be a short hike.

But what you also need to know is that although Italians speak of *trails*, there really is no such thing when it comes to what they call "trekking." Rather, what they mean by *trail* is that a group of disorganized volunteers have designated general and vague directions by piling up little stacks of rocks into primitive markers. But these piles are confusing, in part because you're already traveling through a boulder field. It's not obvious which is the next pile of stones, and sometimes there are multiple little routes set up by different bands of enthusiastic volunteers. Thus, my progress up and over the crest toward the precipitous coast that promised such fabulous views over the Cala d'Inferno went slower, and was hotter, than expected, and I kept tearing my legs on those nasty plants. And there was no shade, because the plants were too starved for water to bother with height.

And that's where things got interesting. I lost my way among those primitive markers in that sunbaked land. I knew vaguely that the coast was on my left, but things had become really steep. And it had gotten really hot. And soon I was out of water. By now I was breathing hard, and my heart-rate was elevated, and I was starting to get dizzy. And that's when I felt something switch on inside: I felt myself move into a different mode of being, a more animal-like state. I had come out as a tourist, in shorts, eager to look at a landscape, taking it in with a painter's eye, but now I had given up caring about looks and landscapes, and even my legs. I needed water. And it was increasingly hard to think. My brain had gone Hemingway on me. Water. Shade. Scuttle, scuttle. Breathing hard. Need rest. Find shade. Get water. I was moving into almost a pure state of animal existence. And I knew I was on the verge of heat stroke. But no one knew where I was. Especially not me. I was three hours of pathless walking from anyone. And that's when I had to admit to myself: I could die here. My brain could just bake to death, and I didn't even know how to call the Italian police. And wouldn't it be embarrassing to have to be airlifted out of this scrub brush, anyway?

It was right around this time that my wife sent me a text:

"How's it going?"

I thought for a while. What do I say? "I'm hiding in fourteen square inches of shade to try to get my heart-rate down from a fatal level"?

Maybe not.

I wrote: "Um. I'm kind of struggling. Drank all my water. Accidentally took a long cut."

She wrote back: "Oh babe. Are you okay?"

I had to explain: "My phone is almost dead. I'll have to turn it off. I'll text you back in thirty minutes, if I make it."

After another hour of this animal-level existence, I did make it to the coast. I looked down from the top of a two-hundred-foot cliff to watch the gem-green water, lifted by swelling waves and pulled up against the jagged rocks where it sloshed up into spray.

It was everything I had hoped for—a glorious and intense symphony of the world's primal elements: heat and water, air and earth. In fact, standing there (maybe this was my impending heatstroke?), I found myself wanting to leap, to immerse myself into that spacious valley of water and rock. I knew, of course, it would be my death, and I wasn't suicidal, but, still, it felt like something was calling me, something alluring and benevolent. It was along this coast that I found an ancient hut of stone. Had it been an ancient shelter for a medieval watchman? Or maybe it was a hermitage for some unknown saint who kept all-night vigils while praying to the stars? I crawled in through the tiny entrance—people were a lot smaller back then—and instantly felt that it was at least twenty degrees cooler. Pure, dark shade. The floor of the hut was wet and muddy. I leaned my back against the cool stones. I closed my eyes and smiled. And then I smiled at my smiling.

Meanwhile, my poor wife was back in our apartment. She later told me that she had been praying in the bathroom, kneeling on those hard marble panels ever-present in Italian bathrooms, so that the kids wouldn't be afraid. And it just so happened that after I stumbled out of the ancient hermitage to head downhill, I heard people, for the first time in four hours, coming up the mountain. A French couple, called Marisa and Cedric, gave me a liter of water and saved my life. Clinging to that water, I struggled down hill over the next two hours through wayless scrub, eventually coming down into the valley and finding a dumpy town, where I hobbled my way over to the most mediocre bar in all of Italy. But it didn't matter. I felt like Odysseus on first seeing Ithaka! I was smiling at the waiters. And I looked so bad—legs covered in blood and clothes stained in sweat and mud—that they made me sit away from the well-groomed customers. But I just kept smiling at everyone, and they kept looking at me with suspicion, turning away to avoid eye contact. I ate a basket of gummy bread, drank a bottle of carbonated water, and then walked down to the coast to lean slowly forward and fall into the water, letting its stinging salt clean my wounds and wipe away my filth. It was the greatest bath I have ever taken.

You'll note the paradox: I had come to Sardinia, crossed international boundaries, dodged waves of Covid policies, endured dozens of Q-tips stuck deeply up my nose, spent thousands of dollars, suffered cancellations and re-bookings, and endured hours on the phone with random, unhelpful, hostile, very British employees: all in order to come sit in the mud of a stone hut?

Yes.

And I loved it. I loved it so much that I'd gladly do it all over again, provided that I could secure my wife's agreement. And that's when I began wondering: is there something wrong with me?

Very likely.

But, according to C. S. Lewis, at least not in this regard. Indeed, it seems that I had accidentally stumbled upon what Lewis thought was the fundamental characteristic of beauty: that is, when we encounter beauty, it is almost always accompanied by a strange note of sorrow, a sorrow that arises because beauty feels like something *over there*, something external to me. And in my gazing upon it, what I find myself wanting is not just to *see* beauty, but to *be* beauty, to make that which I see (or hear or read) become a permanent part of my being. I want to make that thing *out there* something *in here*. I don't want to be a tourist. I want to be local. I don't want to look at a beautiful country; I want to speak its language, understand the subtlety of its jokes, feel its feelings, hunger for its food, and use its curse words. As one of my teachers says, "I don't want just to see beauty, I want to eat it." Or to put it another way: I don't want to stream, I want to download. Here are Lewis's own magical words to describe this desire, taken from his hauntingly beautiful sermon "Weight of Glory":

> God has given us the Morning Star already: you can go and enjoy the gift on many fine mornings if you get up early enough. What more, you may ask, do we want? Ah, but we want so much more—something the books on aesthetics take little notice of. But the poets and the mythologies know all about it. We do not want merely to *see* beauty, though, God knows, even that is bounty enough. We want something else which can hardly be put into words—to be united with the beauty we see, to pass into it, to receive it into ourselves, to bathe in it, to become part of it.[2]

2    C. S. Lewis, "Weight of Glory," in *Essay Collection and Other Short Pieces*, ed. Lesley Walmsley (San Francisco: HarperSan-Francisco, 2000), 104.

And this is exactly what I had accidentally inflicted on myself in Sardinia. The distance between me and the landscape had been erased. I had been reduced to an experience of pure elemental conditions, and I loved it, because I was no longer a tourist. I was local. More than local. Its ecosystem had been written onto my body. After multiple hours in that sun-bleached wilderness, I had come to value water like those plants *out there*. I scurried from one patch of shade to the next, leaving pieces of my skin behind on every branch. I was no longer human. I was a lizard: a Mediterranean salamander. I had shed 87% of my rationality and loved doing so, because the gap between what I saw *out there* and what I held *within* had begun to close. I was being reunited, as Lewis puts it, with something in the universe from which I had been alienated before:

> Apparently, then, our lifelong nostalgia, our longing to be reunited with something in the universe from which we now feel cut off, to be on the inside of some door which we have always seen from the outside, is no mere neurotic fancy, but the truest index of our real situation. And to be at last summoned inside would be both glory and honour beyond all our merits and also the healing of that old ache.[3]

The bad news, according to Lewis, is this: in our natural human condition, we are alienated from that which we want to belong to most, so that, even in the midst of the most poignant experience of beauty, there is an unexpected note of sorrow, because we feel the gap between us and it. And even as we experience beauty, we feel like we are being pulled away from it, dragged back into the flow of time, losing the ability to be

---

3    Lewis, 104.

fully attentive to it, flowing along the river of time while beauty remains *over there,* on the sublime and tranquil coast of eternity.

And this hurts.

But the good news is that I *can,* to whatever extent, close the gap between myself and the beauty *out there*. I *can,* to whatever extent, get it—a little bit—into the marrow of my bones. I can, to whatever extent, eat beauty.

And how?

Through literature, of course! And painting, and architecture, and music. And liturgy. Indeed, for Lewis, this was even *the* fundamental drive of ancient myth. We compliment our ancestors, with infinite condescension, believing that they were trying to take their first primitive steps toward science, toward being us, but Lewis thought ancient mythology was instead driven by this spiritual longing to metabolize the beautiful. Because we want to be united with beauty, he says, "we have peopled air and earth and water with gods and goddesses and nymphs and elves—that, though we cannot, yet these projections can, enjoy in themselves that beauty, grace, and power of which Nature is the image."[4]

We can find an example of what Lewis had in mind when we consider the story of Glaucus, as told in Ovid's *Metamorphoses*. Although the Roman poet generally prefers depressing tales of tragic violence and loss, this is one of his few charming stories. One day a simple fisherman, Glaucus, is fishing in a new location and brings in a good haul of fish. Having pulled in his heavy net, he lays his fish on the preternaturally bright green grass. Bu after just a few minutes, the fish, to his astonishment, magically come back to life and flip-flop their way back down to the sea. Glaucus is confused but suspects that the grass on which they had been set is somehow sacred, and so he creeps over to take a bite of it himself. Here is Ovid's description of what happens next, written from the

---

4    Lewis, 104.

perspective of Glaucus:

> I stood dumbfounded, for a while not believing it, searching for the cause. Had some god done it, or the juice of some herb? "Yet what herb has such power?" I asked, and gathering some herbage in my hand, I bit what I had gathered with my teeth. My throat had scarcely swallowed the strange juice, when suddenly I felt my heart trembling inside me, my breast seized with yearning for that other element. Unable to hold out for long, crying out: "Land, I will never return to, goodbye!" I immersed my body in the sea.… Immediately streams from every side poured their waters over my head. So much I can tell of you of those marvellous things, so much of them I remember: then my mind knew no more. When later I came to, my whole body was altered from what I was before, and my mind was not the same.[5]

Ovid relates, then, the metamorphosis of Glaucus, how he went from human to sea god, how, within, he found an inner longing for new and unaccustomed depths, a new hunger to swim with new speed and to explore levels of reality he had never previously even thought of. And he doesn't just want to know about them—to know what they are called and where they are located, to know their longitude and latitude; rather, he wants to belong to them and have them belong to him. He doesn't want to stream the experience: he wants to download it. So Glaucus says goodbye to the ordinary land and the prosaic life that once sustained him, and throws himself into the sea. But what I especially

---

5    Ovid, *Metamorphoses*, Ovid Collection, The University of Virginia Electronic Texts Center, accessed October 31, 2024, https://ovid.lib.virginia.edu/trans/Metamorph13.htm. I am using Kline's translation of Book XIII. 898–968.

like about Ovid's story is that he relates the transformation from the inside out, from what film makers call "the point-of-view shot." Glaucus munches on the magical grass and, Ovid tells us, while doing so he feels his "heart trembling inside" and his "breast seized with yearning for that other element." It's so tactile. Ovid tells us how the cool water felt on his skin when he was "immersed" in the sea and how "streams from every side poured their waters over [his] head." This inner yearning, this interior passion, finds its expression in a tactile, sensuous, palpable, haptic, and exterior experience. You can see why this story charmed Dante, who, a millennium after Ovid, pulled it out of his memory and used it as the best image for what his own tale of transformation in *Paradiso* would feel like.

If we keep in mind that literature is driven by the desire to close the gap between *what I see* and *what I am*, then we will be more patient with the old authors, especially in those passages which might otherwise seem slow or strange or overly rhetorical. Take, for instance, a wonderful and curious passage in another author of the ancient Mediterranean, Homer, who, in his *Odyssey*, doesn't give us right away the burly hero we had been waiting for. We don't meet the great warrior until Book V, and even then, he's going to be put through a series of tests through which the celebrity conqueror will come to love, with every drop of blood in his body, the lowly and humble things he had been too arrogant to even notice in his younger life. For instance, when his home-made craft, built with borrowed tools, is ruined by a storm at sea, Odysseus is obliged to cling to the wreckage for three days before seeing landfall. But there is one last obstacle before arrival: the shore is made up of jagged rocks. Having noted the peril of the coast, Odysseus must swim parallel to that shore until he finds the mouth of a river, at which point he will be able to climb safely onto shore. But before he can do all that, he is nearly destroyed by a great surge of water that tosses him up onto the jagged rocks of a reef. The wave carried him against the rough rock face,

and there his skin would have been taken off, his bones crushed together,

had not the gray-eyed goddess Athene sent him an inkling,

and he frantically caught hold with both hands on the rock face

and clung to it, groaning, until the great wave went over. This one

he so escaped, but the backwash of the same wave caught him

where he clung and threw him far out in the open water.

As when an octopus is dragged away from its shelter

the thickly-clustered pebbles stick in the cups of the tentacles,

so in contact with the rock the skin from his bold hands

was torn away.[6]

Odysseus did get to his river mouth, eventually. And when he did, he staggered out of the water and "lay down again in the rushes and kissed the grain-giving soil." He knows that he is so weak and exhausted that even a chilly wind in the morning will finish him off, and so he sets about looking for shelter:

[H]e went to look for the wood and found it close to the water

in a conspicuous place, and stopped underneath two bushes

that grew from the same place, one of shrub, and one of wild olive,

and neither the force of wet-blowing winds could penetrate these

nor could the shining sun ever strike through with his rays, nor yet

---

6    Homer, *The Odyssey of Homer* (New York: Harper Perennial, 2007), V. 425–35. I am using Richmond Lattimore's translation.

> could the rain pass all the way through them, so close together
>
> were they grown, interlacing each other; and under these now Odysseus
>
> entered, and with his own hands heaped him a bed to sleep on,
>
> making it wide, since there was great store of fallen leaves there,
>
> enough for two men to take cover in or even three men
>
> in the winter season, even in the very worst kind of weather.
>
> Seeing this, long-suffering great Odysseus was happy,
>
> and lay down in the middle, and made a pile of leaves over him.
>
> As when a man buries a burning log in a black ash heap....[7]

The King of Ithaka, Agamemnon's Four-Star General of Joint Operations, ancient civilization's Most Interesting Man in the World, crawls into a pile of leaves and covers himself up. And then he smiles, and smiles at his smiling.

Throughout Odysseus's landing scene, then, we have rock and water and dirt and storm, but we also have curiously specific details. Why does Odysseus go to sleep underneath a "wild olive"? What is the octopus doing here, with his little cups full of pebbles, himself desperately trying to cling to the reef while being dragged along by the heavy water? The brilliance of the octopus and the wild olive is that they are *not* symbols, allegories, or types. Instead, by them, Homer gets us into the picture. It is by them that we can live out Odysseus's tenacity and later feel his exhausted gratitude. It is one thing to say that Odysseus held on, another to say that the palms of his hands (a very sensitive part of the body: we can feel that) were lacerated as he held on. But it is another thing still to say he held on analogously to how an irrational octopus holds on. In this desperate struggle, wily, scheming, calculating Odysseus is momentarily, and uncharacteristically, left without

---

7    Homer, V. 475–88

any thoughts or designs at all. In an unreflecting act of pure instinctual drive, he clings to life as tenaciously as an animal that merely possesses such an impulse. And later he will collapse, so fatigued that a pile of leaves will fill him with a deep sense of gratitude. He will feel like he is embracing the earth. By these metaphors and images, we get as close as possible to a total immersion into the mythically perilous sea and the reassuring stability of earth. Indeed, in this scene, we find the master of archaic poetry weaving the weft of the human heart into the warp of the universe. Homer has closed the gap.

---

But in addition to this poetic "stickiness" that comes from the use of natural and sensuous metaphors, poets and artists have used all kinds of other devices to try to close the gap between the beautiful *out there* and who I am *in here*. Words, like music, proceed one after the other in time. For us, they move, in unceasing motion, from left to right. And yet, there are a number of poets who try to disrupt this temporal cadence of language, to "still" this temporal flow, and to "spatialize" their words, to slow them down, make them linger, freeze them in memory. George Herbert, for instance, set some of his poems to take on graphic shapes (such as "The Altar" or "Easter Wings"), seemingly because by making us *see* these poems as sculptures, we feel the content differently, more solidly, more spatially. And if you could imitate altars and wings in verse, as Herbert did, why not also liturgical vessels? Robert Southwell designed an extraordinary poem, "Christ's Bloody Sweate," whose meaning does indeed unfold, as you would expect, from left to right, but it also meaningfully moves from top to bottom, as well as diagonally, from top left to bottom right:

| Fatt soyle, | full springe, | sweete olive, | grape of blisse |
| That yeldes, | that streames, | that powres, | that dost distil |
| Untild, | undrawne, | unstampde, | untouchd of presse |
| Deare fruit, | cleare brooks, | fayre oyle, | sweete wine at will |

Thus Christ unforc'd preventes in shedding bloode,

The whippes the thornes the nayles the speare and roode.[8]

In other words, it's a poem whose meaning irradiates out in all directions, so that Peter Davidson has compared it to a Baroque monstrance.[9] The clusters of images, however, which can be combined in various ways, resist the easy narrative of Christ's agony and create a time-stilling pattern.

This "spatialization of the temporal," in which we make our words feel to be, in whatever capacity, sculptural, is such a powerful technique that many critics in mid-twentieth-century America wondered if it might be *the* most important feature of lyric poetry, the beating heart of lyric itself. In fact, in the middle of the twentieth century, there was a scholarly craze to claim that poetry was at its most poetic when most spatial. Scholars, such as Murray Krieger, had in mind, not just figure poems, like those mentioned above, but also poems of *ekphrasis;* that is, those moments where poets use words to describe paintings or sculptures and, thus, implicitly make a connection between the way they do their verbal art and what they are looking at. The shield of Achilles from *Iliad* 18, Dido's decorated temple in the *Aeneid*, Dante's carved floor and wall on the terrace of

---

8    Robert Southwell, "Christ's Bloody Sweate," in *The Complete Poems of Robert Southwell, S.J.* (London: Robson and Sons, 1872), 137–38.

9    Peter Davidson, *The Universal Baroque* (Manchester: Manchester University Press, 2007), 178.

the prideful, W. H. Auden's "Musee des Beaux Arts," and Gjertrud Schnackenberg's "Supernatural Love" are all brilliant examples of what Krieger in the 1960s called "the still movement of poetry."[10] Krieger went so far as to assert that the secret desire of all poetry is to create within itself "the sense of roundedness" (like Keats's Grecian urn) by using "all sorts of repetitions, echoes, complexes of internal relations" to convert "chronological progression into simultaneity" to change the "temporally unrepeatable flow into eternal recurrence." Poetry, then, seeks to take time's "linear movement" and turn it into a circle, and, thus, through "miracles performed in time…thanks to the powers of poetic discourse" make "a specially frozen sort of aesthetic time."[11]

Above all, Krieger has Keats's "Ode on a Grecian Urn" in mind, considered by him to be not only the greatest example of *ekphrasis*, but, as such, the most perfect lyric poem. As Keats describes his imaginary and perfect Greek vase, he calls it the "bride of quietness" and the child of "silence and slow time." Keats says that the figures painted on the vase—such as the youth playing music and the Apollo-like lover reaching out for his Daphne, as in Bernini's statue—are superior to us mere mortals. Why? Because while we experience passion, too, we of course get tired out by it and fade; but the figures on the vase remain still, eternal, and "cannot fade." They belong to this other world of stillness and slow time. And yet, the poet is intent on reaching into this world, baptizing his words within this still river of eternity. This is why he addresses his characters and tries to move into their plane of being. He praises them, talks to us about them, but, most importantly, tries to get their still "roundedness" into *his language* through rhymes, patterns, and repetitions: in short, the magic of poetic devices. And, of course, the poem ends with its

---

10   Murray Krieger, "The Ekphrastic Principle and the Still Movement of Poetry; or Laokoon Revisited," in *The Play and Place of Criticism* (Baltimore: Johns Hopkins University Press, 2019), 105–28.

11   Krieger, 105.

famous, rounded, circular tautological claim, spoken by the vase to our linear world:

> Ah, happy, happy boughs! that cannot shed
>
>> Your leaves, nor ever bid the Spring adieu;
>
> And, happy melodist, unwearied,
>
>> For ever piping songs for ever new;
>
> More happy love! more happy, happy love!
>
>> For ever warm and still to be enjoy'd,
>
>>> For ever panting, and for ever young;
>
> All breathing human passion far above,
>
>> That leaves a heart high-sorrowful and cloy'd,
>
>> A burning forehead, and a parching tongue.

> Thou, silent form, dost tease us out of thought
>
> As doth eternity: Cold Pastoral!
>
>> When old age shall this generation waste,
>
>> Thou shalt remain, in midst of other woe
>
> Than ours, a friend to man, to whom thou say'st,
>
>> "Beauty is truth, truth beauty,—that is all
>
>> Ye know on earth, and all ye need to know."[12]

We see, then, that as Keats meditates on this "cold" landscape of eternity, with its leaves and music that cannot end, and with its youths whose beauty cannot fade, he

---

12    Keats, "Ode on a Grecian Urn," Poetry Foundation, accessed October 15, 2024, https://www.poetryfoundation.org/poems/44477/ode-on-a-grecian-urn. I am quoting here lines 21–30 and lines 44–50.

desperately tries to get some of the beauty that is *out there*, some of that eternal stillness, into himself, into his own words. Thus, Keats's words are drawn into the pure world of geometry: his lines are shaped into five metrical iambic feet that make ten-syllable verses. But these lines of iambic pentameters are further built out into five stanzas, each of which has ten lines, and each stanza— yes, you guessed it!—has five rhyme words that follow the abab cdecde pattern. What we have, then, is a poem in which fickle, flowing, frivolous, time-bound feelings and passing utterances of sound are stilled and rendered spatial, sculptural, and rounded off into an intricate, patterned temple of fives within tens and tens within fives. Keats does for language what the ancient Greeks had done for their temples.

If power to render time "still" is one of the ways that literature tries to close the gap between itself and what it looks at, then we don't necessarily have to seek out poems that look like what they talk about (figure poems) or even poems of *ekphrasis*. We can also look for any poem that stacks layers of metaphors (like some medieval chalice or reliquary, densely set with gems) and forms clusters of dazzling images which, thereby, slow the "flow" of the temporal narrative and make it stand still ("spatializing the temporal"). Take George Herbert's "Prayer," as an example:

> Prayer the church's banquet, angel's age,
> God's breath in man returning to his birth,
> The soul in paraphrase, heart in pilgrimage,
> The Christian plummet sounding heav'n and earth
> Engine against th' Almighty, sinner's tow'r,
> Reversed thunder, Christ-side-piercing spear,
> The six-days world transposing in an hour,

> A kind of tune, which all things hear and fear;
>
> Softness, and peace, and joy, and love, and bliss,
>
> Exalted manna, gladness of the best,
>
> Heaven in ordinary, man well drest,
>
> The milky way, the bird of Paradise,
>
> Church-bells beyond the stars heard, the soul's blood,
>
> The land of spices; something understood.[13]

The poem is not physically shaped like prayer (any attempt to do that would belong on the bumper of a pick-up truck), but its dense use of metaphors and different names for prayer does create a super-saturated hyper-language, one that feels likes it is reaching beyond mere time-bound narrative into the stillness of eternity, which is what prayer is supposed to do. Each new image refines the previous. Prayer is like if you could squeeze a whole week into a single hour. No, prayer is like seeing a tropical bird in the middle of your European garden ("bird of Paradise"). No, prayer is like if you suddenly noticed that many big, booming bells—like those that ring on Easter Sunday in Rome—had been ringing somewhere "beyond the stars."

------

This, then, is the good news. To some extent, to some measure, we *can* overcome our time-bound mortality in the effort to draw closer to eternity. Literature—and her sisters arts—is driven by the secret desire to close the gap between myself and that beauty *out there*, to get that *into* me, to make beauty not something I simply gaze on, but something I feel palpably, sensuously, tangibly—something that is weighty and heavy and embodied

---

13   George Herbert, "Prayer (I)," Poetry Foundation, accessed November 4, 2024, https://www.poetryfoundation.org/poems/44371/prayer-i. I here quote the poem in full.

and feels slow and spacious and still and suspended.

This is also the reason why Lewis loved, so much, the metaphor of landscape as a way of trying to capture what reading literature feels like. At once a great walker and a greater reader, he felt—at whatever level—that being spatially immersed within this sensuous world, experienced all in slow time, combined all of the metaphors discussed above in a single dense, layered moment, just like literature does, especially in premodern poetry. For Lewis, the *Odyssey* has the Mediterranean's "clear, bitter brightness that lives in almost every formula," while the haunting and vague longing of Joy, which he got through a book on Norse Mythology, is like that strange, icy sensation you get when you contemplate "pure 'Northerness'" and get a vision of "huge, clear spaces hanging above the Atlantic in the endless twilight of Northern summer, remoteness, severity."[14] After literature and walking, Lewis's third and fourth greatest passions were tobacco and talking, so it's quite telling that Lewis was willing to lay aside both of those activities so they would not interfere with the reception of the complex, multi-sensory experience of landscape. You shouldn't take walks with a friend, he said, "except at rare intervals":

> Walking and talking are two very great pleasures, but it is a mistake to combine them. Our own noise blots out the sounds and silences of the outdoor world; and talking leads almost inevitably to smoking, and then farewell to nature as far as one of our senses is concerned. The only friend to walk with is one (such as I found, during the holidays, in Arthur) who so exactly shares your taste for each mood of the countryside that a glance, a halt, or at most a nudge, is enough to assure us that the

---

14   C. S. Lewis, *Surprised by Joy* (New York: Harcourt Brace and Company, 1984), 145, 73.

pleasure is shared.[15]

Literature, like landscapes, affects us. Landscapes get into us, make our cheeks red and noses cold, our fingers numb.[16] And this is what literature longs for: an embodied world of weight that I can enter into, plunge into, in order that their beauties can get into me. I want to be on the surface of Keats's vase, be immersed in Glaucus's sea, travel as Lewis's silent companion in Surrey, and cling to the reef along with Odysseus and Homer's octopus. It is for this very reason that Lewis compares this complex, multi-sensory, alert but receptive slow-time experience of spaciousness to literature. In this case, he compares the landscape of Surrey to Malory and Spenser:

> Meanwhile, on afternoons and on Sundays, Surrey lay open to me. County Down in the holidays and Surrey in the term—it was an excellent contrast. Perhaps, since their beauties were such that even a fool could not force them into competition, this cured me once and for all of the pernicious tendency to compare and to prefer… Total surrender is the first step toward the fruition of either. Shut your mouth; open your eyes and ears. Take in what is there and give no thought to what might

---

15   Lewis, 142.

16   "The valley twisted away southward into another valley, a train thudded past invisible in a wooded cutting… But I remember more dearly autumn afternoons in bottoms that lay intensely silent under old and great trees, and especially the moment, near Friday Street, when our party (that time I was not alone) suddenly discovered, from recognizing a curiously shaped stump, that we had traveled round in a circle for the last half-hour; or one frosty sunset over the Hog's Back at Guildford. On a Saturday afternoon in winter, when nose and fingers might be pinched enough to give an added relish to the anticipation of tea and fireside, and the whole week end's reading lay ahead, I suppose I reached as much happiness as is ever to be reached on earth. And especially if there were some new, long-coveted book awaiting me" (146–47).

have been there or what is somewhere else. That can come later, if it must come at all… What delighted me in Surrey was its intricacy. My Irish walks commanded large horizons and the general lie of land and sea could be taken in at a glance; I will try to speak of them later. But in Surrey the contours were so tortuous, the little valleys so narrow, there was so much timber, so many villages concealed in woods or hollows, so many field paths, sunk lanes, dingles, copses, such an unpredictable variety of cottage, farmhouse, villa, and country seat, that the whole thing could never lie clearly in my mind, and to walk in it daily gave one the same sort of pleasure that there is in the labyrinthine complexity of Malory or the *Faerie Queene*.[17]

Apparently, reading literature for Lewis was not just an embodied experience, but also one of expansive spaciousness, in which we enjoy a slow-time experience, in the manner similar to how we pass through a landscape that is new to us. And we're especially fortunate that Lewis himself provided the analogy: passing through the autumnal landscape of Surrey felt like reading Spenser! We can conclude this chapter by following up on that lead.

In addition to the *Fairie Queene*, Lewis loved Edmund Spenser's "Epithalamium," which, he thought, with the exception of one stanza, was a perfect poem, indeed, the greatest ode written since Greek antiquity. "Epithalamium" is an example of a now-defunct genre of writing, the wedding or bride song, in which a poet imagines a ceremonial procession of the young woman from her house to the home of her new husband, hence, epi-thalamion (toward the bridal chamber). A chorus of singing bridesmaids accompanies

17   Lewis, 145–46.

the bride through her transition from life as a girl to the life of a married matron.

In Spenser's particular iteration of this genre, he divides up the linear narrative into stanza-long snapshots. For instance, after the introductory stanza, Spenser devotes a block of eighteen lines to the task of bidding the muses to go, before dawn, to wake up his future bride and sing to her songs of joy and cheer. The third stanza zooms out, as it were, bidding all the nymphs and dryads in the surrounding woods to put on festal cheer, as well. Other stanzas zoom in, addressing handmaids or even inanimate parts of the landscape (woods or streams) and asking them to spiritually accompany the new bride. Through a series of stanzas the narrative advances one slow step at a time: the beloved awakes, she dresses, she walks ceremoniously toward the church. In general, there is little narrative content in the poem, and sometimes no action whatsoever occurs in a particular stanza, but all of this zooming out and zooming in is held together by the final line of each stanza. At the end of the first stanza, we read: "So I unto my selfe alone will sing, / The woods shall to me answer and my Eccho ring."[18] The second stanza ends: "Doe ye to her of joy and solace sing, / That all the woods may answer and your eccho ring."[19] In this way, each of the stanzas double back on themselves, slowing down their linear progress, and making a narrative shape more like rippling patterns of water, or like the intricate "fan vaulting" of the so-called Perpendicular style in late Gothic English art which was fashionable during Spenser's day.

We could also compare Spenser's narrative structure—which moves forward but, then, arrests its linearity to loop back upon itself—to the structure of Bach's *St. Matthew's Passion,* which is made up of recitatives: they advance the linear story from the Gospel,

---

18   Edmund Spenser, "Epithalamion," Poetry Foundation, accessed October 29, 2024, https://www.poetryfoundation.org/poems/45191/epithalamion-56d22497d00d4. These are lines 17–18.

19   Spenser, v. 35–36.

but these bits of narrative are punctuated by arias and chorales that circle back to take up something previously mentioned in the recitative, and then meditate on it, musically, in an effort to amplify the piece's emotional power. And once you have eyes for the pattern, you find it everywhere in premodern art: you find it in Ockegum's "Deo Gratias" for thirty-six voices, William Byrd's *Fantasia*, Tallis's "Spem in alium." This is the secret link between premodern "secular" literature and premodern sacred culture. In ritualistic cultures, even secular literature rests uncertainly on the boundary of sacred enterprises. Cultures that love liturgies, litanies, processions, rituals, liturgical hymns, and symbols also love illuminations, "perpendicular style" chapel ceilings, musical "perpetual canons," sonnet cycles, and narratives that are woven together in versified stanzas.

In the meantime, Spenser feels the weight of those learned Greek and Latin poems he took as paradigmatic, and so the English poet uses mythological allusions (invoking the muses, comparing himself to Orpheus, likening his poem to Echo) and alliterations ("dolefull dreriment" and "mishaps to mourn"). He further heightens the poetic quality by stacking up rhetorical techniques, using antithesis and wordplay ("even the greatest did not greatly scorne"), and hyperbaton in almost every single line ("when ye liste your own mishapes to mourn" as opposed to the more normal "when you wish to mourn your own misfortunes"). Spenser, then, is a poet of "slow movement" and "opulence":

> Early before the worlds light giving lampe,
> His golden beame upon the hils doth spred,
> Having disperst the nights unchearefull dampe,
> Doe ye awake, and with fresh lusty hed,
> Go to the bowre of my beloved love,
> My truest turtle dove,

> Bid her awake; for Hymen is awake,
>
> And long since ready forth his maske to move,
>
> With his bright Tead that flames with many a flake,
>
> And many a bachelor to waite on him,
>
> In theyr fresh garments trim.
>
> Bid her awake therefore and soone her dight,
>
> For lo the wished day is come at last,
>
> That shall for al the paynes and sorrowes past,
>
> Pay to her usury of long delight:
>
> And whylest she doth her dight,
>
> Doe ye to her of joy and solace sing,
>
> That all the woods may answer and your eccho ring.[20]

What is incredible is that, to describe this opulent, spacious, sensuous "slowness," Spenser would have used the word "amplification," a word also used to describe the art of modernity. But for our premodern ancestors "amplification" was different: it was an elaborate unfolding within *space*, as opposed to an increase of the distance between peaks and troughs within *time*. Amplification was not a hyping up, an acceleration of mass, an increase of momentum, but rather the attempt to render a vision "full," generous, abundant, charged with density, alive beyond any expectation. Amplification wasn't connected to "amps," "amperes," and getting "amped up," but to "ampleness." It was cornucopia, gracious fullness, generous abundance. It was a spatial phenomenon, not a temporal one. For us, good writing needs to be stripped down, deliver impact, download huge amounts of kilobytes. For our ancestors, language could luxuriate, grow abundant, by using those

---

20  Spenser, v. 19–36.

very tropes and schemes which we find so cloying. Spenser doesn't want to rush through or create impact. He wants to *slow* time, overcome time—spatialize the temporal. He wants this poetic moment to feel dense, holy, and alive. Rather than rushing forward, he wants time to slow down, take its time, reach down into the depths within, while creating a sense of generous and slow spaciousness.

# CHAPTER 3

## DOWN THE RABBIT HOLE

I cited the passages from Lewis in the previous chapter because I thought them to be evocative articulations of the relationship between literature and landscape, but we cannot continue on in this flushed and sanguine encomium of premodern literature without pausing to notice a note of anxiety in Lewis, what you might call a change from a major to minor key. Shortly after praising the unique beauty of his native Northern Ireland, Lewis pauses to reflect on how fortunate he was to grow up as a child without access to cars:

> The deadly power of rushing about wherever I pleased had not been given me. I measured distances by the standard of man, man walking on his two feet, not by the standard of the internal combustion engine. I had not been allowed to deflower the very idea of distance; in return I possessed 'infinite riches' what would have been to motorists 'a little room.' The truest and most horrible claim made for modern transport is that it 'annihilates space.' It does. It annihilates one of the most glori-

ous gifts we have been given. It is a vile inflation which lowers the value

of distance, so that a modern boy travels a hundred miles with less sense

of liberation and pilgrimage and adventure than his grandfather got

from traveling ten.[1]


We have been conditioned to think of any technological advance as an unambig-

uous improvement for our lives, and so we eagerly wait for the next model of phone or

the next generation of car and dutifully upgrade our systems and download the latest

app. The fact that Lewis imagines the possible downsides of labor-saving devices comes

as a surprise, but this is not the only time that Lewis worried about our relationship to

machines. The same theme comes up in *That Hideous Strength* and *Abolition of Man,* as

well as in the lecture he gave when he assumed his academic chair at Cambridge: *De

Descriptione Temporum.* In that lecture, Lewis provocatively claimed that we have less in

common with our grandparents' grandparents, than they had in common with Caesar,

Beowulf, Achilles, or the Pharaohs. He arrives at this stupefying assertion by reflecting on

a fascinating question: what would happen if we spent more time around our machines

than we spent with the natural world? What would happen if machine metaphors got

into our imaginations so deeply that we forgot they were there, and, thus, without us even

knowing it, we began to think and feel about ourselves and our lives and our goals as if

we were machines or work functions, too?

In Lewis's view, this is exactly what happened. As metaphors drawn from classical

mechanics slowly began to penetrate the vocabulary of the residents of the modern

world, eventually even every-day people began to refer to themselves as "consumers" and

"producers" who bring their "labor supply" to "human resource departments" and try,

---

1    C. S. Lewis, *Surprised by Joy* (New York: Harcourt Brace and Company, 1984), 157.

every day, to "optimize their productivity." What is more, Lewis also reflected on how there were shifts within our individual words, so that, sometimes, what had been words of praise for our ancestors became words of condemnation for us, and vice versa. For instance, Lewis wondered why we use the word "stagnation" (a word that has overtones of malarial swamps) for social conditions our ancestors would have praised because of their "permanence." Lewis also asked why it is that when we use the word "primitive," we instantly feel connotations of "clumsiness, inefficiency, barbarity," whereas our ancestors talked of the "primitive church" or the "primitive purity" of a constitution and meant "pure" and "vital." And then my personal favorite: "Why does 'latest' in advertisement mean 'best'?" The answer, according to Lewis, is that now the image of "old machines being superseded by new and better ones" has become for us the controlling archetype in our imagination. Lewis noted that machines and technologies are so important for us as moderns that they began to mark the great milestones of our lives. Along with our marriages and the births of our children, we also remember when we got our first iPhones, just as our grandparents marked out seasons of their lives when the telephone arrived or color television appeared. Indeed, for us, giving our children their first smart phone has become the ritualized initiation into adulthood that has supplanted confirmation, an ordeal of manhood, or bar mitzvah. Lewis was prescient, then: machines are in our brain and our blood and our words and in our air and in our water. Don't we also tell one another that we don't have the bandwidth to worry about that right now, but if you just give me a minute, I'll process what you've said? Or we apologize for reverting back to a default mode; well, that's ok—I guess that's just how you're hardwired. We refer to the assets in our department and worry that we might not have the resources we need to sufficiently maximize our outputs.

In other words, what sets us apart, not just from our grandparents' grandparent's generation, but from all the rest of human history, is what you might call the "psychological internalization" of the mechanization of the world picture—a pretentious phrase perhaps, but it just means this: an expectation has gotten into our blood and our bones and our brains that we must constantly and actively seek to amp up our lives. We implicitly think of our lives as productivity functions, as if the years allotted to us were leased in return for mechanistic efficiency. And it is this expectation, not just of speed but of acceleration and efficiency and elimination of resistance, that

> separates us most sharply from our ancestors and whose absence would strike us as most alien if we could return to their world. Conversely, our assumption that everything is provisional and soon to be superseded, that the attainment of goods we have never yet had, rather than the defense and conservation of those we have already, is the cardinal business of life, would most shock and bewilder them if they could visit ours.[2]

------------

As a scholar of the sixteenth century, Lewis was particularly aware of the details of the changing of world pictures. The story of modernity is, as everyone knows, intimately bound up with the rise of empirical science during the Scientific Revolution, and the Scientific Revolution was itself tied up with new instruments which were used to measure, quantify, and magnify: modern cartography, the clock, the barometer, the telescope, the microscope, linear perspective, and eventually technologies such as the steam engine, the telegram, and industrial machinery. And these instruments were used to get precise measurements, so that the harmonic cosmos of antiquity yielded to the inanimate world of

2    C. S. Lewis, "*De Descriptione Temporum*," in *Selected Literary Essays*, ed. Walter Hooper (Cambridge: Cambridge University Press, 2019), 11.

mechanistic structure of mathematized quantities. This is what historians of science mean by the "mechanization of the world picture": that is, the more we used machines—like clocks and telescopes—to study the natural world, the more it looked like a great machine.

It was the legacy of the Enlightenment, though, to explore whether or not this methodology of dividing things into standard units on a grid and then mapping their motions as if they were functions, employed so successfully by physicists to map the natural world, could also be applied to human societies. Especially during the French Enlightenment, a period of Newton-mania, there was a movement to think about human society as if it were a subset of physics. Could we discover the primitive elements…among people? And then chart their mechanistic interactions? And if so, could we then reverse engineer the mechanism to create behavioral technologies which rendered the desired outputs? Apparently so.

Michel Foucault in a famous chapter from *Discipline and Punish* dug up from the archives of seventeenth-century France a series of decrees issued during sporadic outbreaks of the plague that illustrated the first tentative steps of graphing society. If a city was overcome by the plague, then you could deploy a new modern method of graphing human communities as Cartesian grids. First, officials would partition the city into assigned districts and institute a magistrate to oversee each district. Then, the magistrate would appoint a team of street inspectors, who, on the designated day, would force all the families to go indoors. Street inspectors would patrol up and down the lanes to ensure compliance. Anyone who violated the order would be executed. Any street inspector who left his post would be executed. Each family would have its own provisions within, but a small wooden canal was built so that each family could have provisions delivered to them, without having to interact with anyone face to face. Foucault comments: "It is a segmented, immobile, frozen space. Each individual is fixed in his place…. The plague is met by order; its function is to sort out every possible confusion."[3] But, as Foucault goes on to show, what was originally a temporary methodical and rational response to a disaster also gave rise to a "political dream" of "the penetration of regulation into even the smallest details of everyday life through the mediation of the complete hierarchy that assured the capillary function of power…."[4]

Foucault then turned to Jeremy Bentham's *Panopticon*, an Enlightenment book describing a new social technology which could, it was hoped, create permanent conditions of order. Those plague-time regulations didn't have to be temporary; if you had the right technology, you could control people forever. You could create conditions in which people always acted with as much order as they did during plague-time regulations. How?

Bentham imagined building a huge, circular, multi-storied tower, surrounded by a great outer ring like an amphitheater, in which there were many individual cells. The cells ran the length of the outer donut and had two windows: one facing toward the tower, the other facing out, to allow the room to be backlit. The tower would have windows, too, but they would be shielded by blinds, with the result that the prisoners in the cells could never tell when they were being watched by the guards in the tower. Through this systematic arrangement of parts within space, the designers could project a sense of constant surveillance: a minimum input of manpower with a maximum output of control. The whole thing could, perhaps, be operated by a single guard. The brilliant feature of the device, in addition to its economy, was that it could be re-used in dozens of different ways. You could adapt it to watching workers in a factory. You could adapt it to watching madmen in an insane asylum or children at school. Or it could watch the electronic checkout lanes

---

3    Michel Foucault, *Discipline and Punish: The Birth of the Prison*, trans. Alan Sheridan (New York: Random House, 1995), 195–96.

4    Foucault, 198.

at Walmart. Foucault comments: "The Enlightenment which discovered the liberties, also invented the disciplines." Although the subjects under study differed (the natural versus the social world), the techniques were the same: ignore the interior; sketch out the subject's actions into graphable space; and then—once partitioned, divided, mapped, and graphed—the space could be used, with minimal effort and maximal output, to control the mechanism.

And just as you could mathematize space, dividing it up into unambiguous grids of standardized size and then finding its maximally optimized layout, it turns out you could also mathematize time. Especially in the industrial movement known as Taylorism, time became money. If, as Newton taught, work is force acting over a distance, and power is work over time, then you can increase the power of production by increasing the force or decreasing the time it takes for it to operate. Frederick Winslow Taylor revolutionized production by breaking down the construction of a product into a series of primitive motions. And then, with his little pocket watch, he made meticulous notes of how long it took a man to make *that* single motion or perform *this* particular action. He effectively made a great engine diagram of the workplace, but one in which the gears and axles were made up of people. Of course, having discovered the mechanism, you could then speed up the parts. In this way, Taylor increased a factory owner's "power" because he got more "work" done in less time. Taylor took time and rendered it more efficient; he lowered the resistance of the circuitry: except, in this machine, the work was the "electricity"; and the "electrical wires" that conducted the energy were the lives and actions of human beings.

Little wonder, then, that at the same time Frederick Winslow Taylor was pulling his watch out of his little jacket pocket, there was a new type of man, a new hero, evolving and adapting to this new mechanized habitat. Jules Verne's Phileas Fogg, for instance, was an international phenomenon, who made his author rich and thrilled millions of readers across Europe (and later theater goers and film watchers) who breathlessly followed each installment of his modern, industrial odyssey of transport. For Verne, Fogg's greatness was measured by his ability to exert unfailing, unemotional, and absolutely rational control over any environment. His power was that of the engineer, whose enhanced abilities came from having access to more precise instruments for analysis and more powerful tools for exerting force. While the heroes of the past had been marked by their long-suffering patience (St. Anthony) or their ability to endure the afflictions of fortune (Sir Gawain) or their ability to overcome even natural revulsion in acts of supernatural charity (St. Francis), Fogg commanded admiration because of his ability to make fortune submit to his will. His powers, then, are technical: they are the ability to harness and practically deploy the forces of Newton.

Not only does the up-to-date, forwarding-thinking, progressive man of the future possess a complicated clock which indicates "the hours, the minutes, the seconds, the days, the months, and the years," but he imposes such mathematical discipline on himself that he is "as exactly regulated as a Leroy chronometer."[5] He measures out the seconds of his days and counts his own steps: "He was so exact that he was never in a hurry…and was economical alike of his steps and his motions. He never took one step too many, and always went to his destination by the shortest cut; he made no superfluous gestures."[6] And in the new world, this gives Fogg a competitive advantage, because he can view the world as nothing more than a technical problem in which obstacles can be overcome by exerting more force and having access to better data. He foreshadows the "datafication" of the future. He has self-engineered his own life. Phileas Fogg is Mark Zuckerberg's grandfather.

And so, although Fogg was not a saint, a hermit, a pilgrim, a knight, a founder, a

---

5    Jules Verne, *Around the World in Eighty Days*, trans. George M. Towle (Boston: James R. Osgood and Company, 1876), 5, 9.

6    Verne, 9.

sage, a mystic, or even a wanderer, he was, at least, "the most deliberate person in the world."[7] And the more and more forward-thinking people self-engineered themselves to get ahead, get with the times, and get ahead of the curve, the faster everything began to feel. It began to seem like there was no way of going back. As George Eliot put it in *Middlemarch,* although she wished she could have written like Fielding, who would "chat with us in all the lusty ease of his fine English," she couldn't. The world had changed: "Fielding lived when the days were longer…when summer afternoons were spacious, and the clock ticked slowly in the winter evenings."[8] But Phileas Fogg seems subtle in comparison to the heroes of the twentieth century.

---

In his own way, the very mid-century and very American painter, Roy Lichtenstein, was brave. Or maybe he was just the ultimate sell out. In either case, the classically trained painter, who found himself living in the age of *Mad Men* and who, thus, also found himself living in a world of new money, new speed, and new machismo, came to a difficult realization: everything he had studied at art school no longer made (commercial) sense. In a world of modern machinery and power and speed, the Old Masters didn't garner the same appeal. So he set himself about reforming every major genre of painting, rejecting all of those enduring painterly conventions which had become "stagnant."

Why pretend?

Instead of following the slow, world-building, multi-layered, atmosphere-rendering art of, say, Rubens or Cezanne, Roy Lichtenstein gave "Rabbit" Angstrom (*Rabbit, Run*), Jack Burden (*All the King's Men*), John Wayne, Don Draper (*Mad Men*), and Lane Coutell (from Salinger's "Franny") something they could feel in the glands. He gave them

---

explosions (*Varoom!*); automobiles, ripping through landscapes and annihilating space and outrunning meaning; and testosterone-driven jet fighters, who let the thrill of launching torpedoes run like fire through their nervous systems (*Whaam!*). In short, he made paintings in which amped up actions take place beneath the ironic gaze of the detached observer. In particular, Lichtenstein likes to portray macho men who express their primal masculinity by operating heavy machinery.

In this way, Lichtenstein "updated" painting and put it into motion, but he also streamlined its visual structures. Like the Old Masters, Lichtenstein painted monumentally, on large canvases, but, unlike traditional painters, he intentionally adopted a popular style of representation used for tabloids, advertisements, and comic books: the so-called dot-matrix system. Critics like to refer to his painting as "amped up," and it's a good metaphor; Lichtenstein both increased the voltage (giving us smashing images of explosion or speed) and reduced the resistance of the circuitry (through using bitty dots, as opposed to the old technique of layers of translucent paint). His paintings feel like they've been plugged into an electrical outlet.

And what is more, at the exact same time that Lichtenstein's Hemingway-esque, emotionally distant, tool-using macho men were employing heavy machinery to smack one another with megatons, and at the exact same time that Lichtenstein's emotionally fragile, wilting females looked on, drowning in a bubble bath of their own emotions, John Updike's Rabbit Angstrom, in the opening scene of *Rabbit, Run*, was running away from his loveless marriage. It's not just that Updike's hero is abandoning his wife and child, but it's how he does it: Rabbit jumps into his car, slams on the accelerator, and starts driving through the night. He doesn't know where he's going, and he doesn't know how long he'll be gone, and the more uncertain he is, the faster he goes. Similarly, Robert Penn Warren created a stream-of-consciousness scene in *All the King's Men*, when his Jack Burden jumps into his car and drives from Louisiana to California and back, just to give himself a chance to think. And likewise, Kazuo Ishiguro's butler in *The Remains of the Day* can only really come to terms with the self-inflicted trauma of his life once he has begun a car trip to the coast.

Most recently, Cormac McCarthy—the man who was a mechanic before he became a full-time novelist—gives us some passages in his final novel, *The Passenger*, that try to out-Hemingway Hemingway. For instance, at one point the main character, Bobby, fetches his Maserati from a storage shed. Here's how McCarthy writes it:

> The car had a cloth cover over it and he made his way along the wall to the front and undid the tie-straps and folded the cloth back…and carried it outside and shook it out. Then he folded it up and carried it back in and put in on the shelf at the front of the locker alongside the trickle-charger. He lifted the scuttle and disconnected the clips from the charger and the timer and pulled the wire out through the wheel-well and he checked the oil and the water. Then he dropped the scuttle and came around and wedged himself through the door and put the key in the ignition and pushed the starter button.[9]

The prose, stripped even of punctuation, is broken down into something quite literally made up of the nuts and bolts of composition. At other points, McCarthy gives us the iconic, macho, American male (it is still 1980 in the novel, you see), who obliterates his own self-consciousness through the exercise of the pure power of physics, like some pilot or driver out of a Lichtenstein painting. Take, for instance, when Bobby drives 600

---

9  Cormac McCarthy, *The Passenger* (New York: Alfred A. Knopf, 2022), 157.

miles from New Orleans to Wartburg, Tennessee, in a single evening:

> It was dark by the time he reached Hattiesburg. He had turned on the
> lights at dusk and he drove to the Alabama State line just east of Merid-
> ian in one hour flat. One hundred and ten miles. It was seventy miles to
> Tuscaloosa and the highway was straight and empty except for an oc-
> casional semi and he opened the Maserati up and drove the forty miles
> to Clinton Alabama in eighteen minutes redlining the engine twice at
> what the speedometer logged as a hundred and sixty-five miles an hour.
> By then he thought he'd probably used up most of his luck with the
> state police and the small town speedtraps he'd blown through and he
> motored leisurely through Tuscaloosa and Birmingham and crossed the
> Tennessee State line just outside of Chattanooga five hours and forty
> minutes after leaving New Orleans.[10]

Then, there's Jay Gatsby, Kerouac's road, and, of course, the grandfather of them
all, Phileas Fogg. But my point is this: we moderns seem to feel the forces of physics viscerally, in our bodies, *as beauty*. Speed, force, power, amplification, and acceleration course
through our blood as aesthetic experiences. Our prophet is Phileas Fogg. Our high priest
is Oppenheimer. And he was the man who, as Freeman Dyson put it in the film *The Day
after Trinity*, couldn't have stopped working on the bomb even if he had wanted to:

> I have felt it myself…the glitter of nuclear weapons. It is irresistible if
> you come to them as a scientist. To feel it's there in your hands, to re-

lease this energy that fuels the stars, to let it do your bidding. To perform these miracles, to lift a million tons of rock into the sky. It is something that gives people an illusion of illimitable power, and it is, in some ways, responsible for all our troubles—this, what you might call technical arrogance, that overcomes people when they see what they can do with their minds.[11]

Or, as crazy old prophetic Filippo Marinetti, after too many glasses of absinthe, summed it all up in his 1909 *Founding and Manifesto of Futurism*, we moderns find the forces of technology more "beautiful" than the slow art of the Old Masters: "We affirm that the world's magnificence has been enriched by a new beauty: the beauty of speed. A racing car whose hood is adorned with great pipes, like serpents of explosive breath—a roaring car that seems to ride on grapeshot is more beautiful than the Victory of Samothrace."[12]

But back to Lichtenstein.

Cars and torpedoes and drowning girls were only the beginning for Lichtenstein. Perhaps his greatest achievement was reforming those types of paintings that are *slow* by nature. How do you, after all, amp up a still life? What do you do with a landscape or an interior room view or an arrangement of grapes in a bowl? Armed with his popularizing technique, Lichtenstein set about to update every major genre of painting: a weighty still life of a basket of fruit by, say, Cezanne becomes, for Lichtenstein, a glass of water with lemon; Van Eyck's warm interiors (like that in *The Arnolfini Wedding*) become vacant, clean Manhattan apartments, with mirrors reflecting nothing; while the traditional portrait

---

11   As cited in Bill Joy's famous *Wired* article "Why the Future Doesn't Need Us."

12   Filippo Marinetti, "The Founding and Manifesto of Futurism," Italian Futurism, accessed November 21, 2024, https://www.italianfuturism.org/manifestos/foundingmanifesto/.

becomes an image of some young woman receiving devastating news while projecting a calm exterior. Lichtenstein even vernacularized Pablo Picasso and Jackson Pollack, who don't look nearly so angsty when executed in the dot-matrix style. In short, he gave us a new kind of "*Masterpiece*," and it made sense within the cosmic imagination of modernity: a world made up of huge amounts of cold and vacant space in which bits of passive matter are moved by external waves of energy until they collide, form new objects, and then break down. Human lives are no different. Invulnerable and violent men speed through life, collide in melodramatic relationships, and ricochet away from the emotional wreckage.

Then there are the landscapes. By reducing the number of colors and the delicacy of balance, Lichtenstein gives us landscapes that reflect back to us only what our emotions bring (look at his *Sunset*). And that is why his paintings feel so comfortable. "100% you." They are so much more familiar than a Rubens. In one of the most memorable teaching moments of my life, I put a slide up before my students, in which I showed a Rubens landscape and a Lichtenstein landscape next to one another, explaining how one represents the slow, iconic cosmos of the Platonic tradition, and one represents the modern cosmic imaginary. My student, Isaac—one of the most honest and fun students I've ever had—yelled out: "Ok, fine! I admit it! I know I shouldn't, but I like Lichtenstein's image more than the one by Rubens!" A huge debate followed in which he got most of the class to admit that, although the Rubens possesses a noticeable complexity of figure and color and layers of background, it feels strangely "flat" and "dull" next to Lichtenstein. Lichtenstein's paintings are plugged into an electrical outlet, and next to the glowing screen, Rubens seems dull.

And this is where all this begins to get a little scary.

If I am right—that next to the high-voltage, amped up paintings of Lichtenstein, the layered and still paintings of the Old Masters (like Rubens) feel *slow*—then we have an interesting problem. It's not that paintings by Rubens have lost their beauty; it's just that our ability to love them, to see them, to feel them, to enter into them has evaporated. We, like Lichtenstein's machine-users, come at them with so much speed and force that they seem slow to us. Temporal amplification has replaced spatial amplification.

And if this is happening with our visual arts, could it also be happening with our music and our poetry? Could it be that I don't have eyes to see beauty, even when it stands in front of me? Indeed, Lewis wondered, is it theoretically possible that we could so perfectly internalize this mechanistic paradigm, and so perfectly immerse ourselves into the world of speed, that we can't read ancient literature anymore? If I bring speed with me, can I feel space? Can we get moving so fast that the literature of our ancestors just feels…slow?

I think this is exactly what is happening. But to explain why I think that is the case, I'll have to tell another story, about another island.

# CHAPTER 4

## DISAPPEARING LANDSCAPES:
## WHAT OUR SELFIES ARE DOING TO OUR SELVES

Those who travel a lot, or at least who travel to the same place often, forget what it is like to feel scared and strange and alien and foreign in an exotic land. It's not at all the kind of feeling you would call "pleasant." If you could bottle the feeling and then try to sell it, no one would buy it. It is one of confusion, tiredness, and anxiety, in which you just want to go hide and be left alone.

I had forgotten this feeling myself. I had it at 19, when I first went abroad, but as I kept going back to England and Italy almost every year after, those strong feelings were more and more diluted with every trip.

But when I visited Iceland, it all came back: anxiety, disorientation, confusion, excitement.

Iceland is, indeed, very foreign. Major highways narrow to one-lane bridges, and paved roads end in gravel lanes with hardly any warning—just a sign: "Malbik Endar." In the western part of the island, the landscape is strange, apocalyptic, open, and void of all but a few emaciated trees. Channels of steam break out of the ground and shoot up. In the south, the skies are open, like they are in Texas, but flocks of fat geese and tiny little sheep—they look like small dogs—move among fields that are intensely green, almost blue, as they are in Gloucestershire. And water is everywhere: falling, cutting through gorges, steaming from the ground, leaping off of steep cliffs in hundreds of unnamed falls that would serve as the heart of a state park anywhere else.

Then there are strange birds, like the Icelandic oystercatcher. He is black on his head and wings, with a long, thin orange beak. But when he is startled, his first seconds of flight look like an explosion, because when he stretches out he reveals a white belly and underwings.

As you try to take all of this in—ugly, steaming boulder fields; startling explosive flights; the cutting and falling of water; roads suddenly plunging into nothing—it creates a bizarre experience of confusion and foreignness, not unlike nausea. It's not pleasant. It is related to what romantic poets and painters called the "sublime": that pleasant horror or heaviness you experience at the foot of a lofty and aloof mountain, or the oppressive awe you experience at the top of a waterfall that remains indifferent to your small presence. To tell the truth, after I had been in Iceland for a few hours, I wanted to go home. I felt sleepy and nervous and confused.

But travel is akin to listening to concert music: you pass through landscapes like you pass through soundscapes, in *time*. If you have ever found yourself sitting in an organ concert, you sometimes wonder to yourself, what am I doing here? Why am I listening to these strange patterns of sound? But then the organist comes upon some delicious passage; it arises and then melts back into the ocean of sound whence it emerged, like a wave that returns to the sea. The point is now clear: the whole composition was made to provide the context for *those* ten seconds of transparency. It's a breakthrough, a falling, a gliding. We don't travel in pursuit of anxiety, of course, but you can't have the breakthrough without the prior disorientation. As your trip unfolds in time, as you move across the landscape and slowly become less anxious of the new and strange, you have a moment in which the radically foreign emerges and presents itself to you in all of its distant glory. This happened to me, as I was hiking up to see a waterfall, Skógafoss, the mighty waterfall in the south.

The river Skógá flows down through mountain highlands, and as it descends, it picks up speed by tumbling down two dozen minor waterfalls. As it rushes through its gorge, it gains additional water, contributed by innumerable small streams that also tumble down small waterfalls over the walls of the gorge. But then the Skógá, with added volume and new speed, approaches the end of its riverbed, holds its breath for a moment, and then recklessly hurls itself over the edge of its known world.

Millions of gallons—imagine an Olympic swimming pool falling from a skyscraper, every second—precipitously fall, gaining ever more speed, before magnificently smashing into the rocks and water below. The water is pulverized into a fine mist, and so the site of impact is hidden in spray, veiled, like some natural liturgy. But then the mist is lifted upward by a steady wind off the ocean. It rises in immense, spiraling turbines that ascend all the way back up to the top of the fall, like clouds of incense.

Once at the top, if you look down, you will see thousands of birds who roost in little crevices in the rocks, like hermits in cells who want to be close to the source of power. Every now and then, they leap out of their little caves and let themselves fall before spreading their wings. They don't have to flap, because the spray-filled shockwave from below sustains their flight. They simply hover there, like one of those mosaics of an angel on the ceiling of a Byzantine church. Meanwhile, if you look up, you will see a mountain face so peculiarly chiseled by rain and wind that it looks like a visage. It exerts—there is no other word for it—a sense of weight, psychological weight that pushes down on you.

As I said, the Romantics would have called this an experience of the "sublime": an experience on the edge of your vocabulary. You can't stop looking, suspended in a wordless gaze. At some point, you know, you must go away, but you also don't want to leave. And so in a feeble effort to remain there forever, you snap a picture and, disappointed with the results, look one last time, longingly, hoping somehow that this sight will imprint itself on your mind forever. And then you leave, knowing the truth: this cannot be forever.

For me, the whole experience was unexpectedly like attending a liturgy—a Byzantine Rite or Orthodox Divine Liturgy, or Evensong in Oxford, or a Catholic Easter Vigil. Very often, the poems and prayers that make up the ceremony do not function like you would think they should. The "Exultet," for instance, the long poem sung at the beginning of a Catholic Easter Vigil on Holy Saturday, does not proceed in a linear way, but rather creates a huge web of associations of light and candles and fire. There are passages in the poem in which the poet turns from contemplating the pillar of fire from the Old Testament, to praising the very candle used within the ceremony, which leads him to meditate on how bees once made the wax which became the candle. Liturgies, then, are webs of words, as opposed to linear plot lines, and as they contemplate what they perform, they seem to slow time down. In a similar way, before the waterfall, I kept having a strange feeling that I was standing in front of a *natural* liturgy, in which a waterfall, veiling itself in a screen of mist, was attended by its hovering, aerial acolytes, who hurled themselves from rocks in perpetual adoration.

My response was one of hushed reverence and a deep desire to be still.

And this, I think, is why I wasn't prepared for what I found below, at the foot of the mountain, where, at the site of impact, a weird tourist ritual was unfolding. For whatever reason, every single visitor feels the need to take one of two pictures:

**Option (1):** Stand on a rock 200 feet in front of the site of collision and then jump up and extend your limbs in all directions. In this way, with the waterfall safely behind you, it might look to the eye of the camera that you are falling (insert emotional reaction here: haha).

**Option (2):** Lean to the side and stretch out your arms, holding them vertically. In this way, you will look like you are holding the waterfall within your hands.

On another occasion, and at a different site, I watched in disbelief as one woman didn't even look at the view with her eyes. Glowering, she lumbered up to the site with loose, bored limbs, staring at her phone the whole time, and then stopped, turned around, posed, smiled brilliantly, and took her selfie. As soon as that was over, her downcast look returned, and she moved back toward the car to drive sullenly away, without even having looked at the natural beauty with her own eyes. Her whole "experience" took sixty seconds. I counted.

Why do we travel thousands of miles to crop the exotic and fit it into our own dimensions? Why do we domesticate the sites we profess admiration for? We conform them to our own image, and then we upload the experience into feeds and post it, in order to commodify the encounter with the wonderful. In other words, we transform a qualitative experience of beauty into a quantified one, the value of which I then judge in the currency of "likes." Here's *me* in front of a lake, *me* in front of a funny sign, *me* in front of *me*…*me*…"100% you." But this obliterates the possibility of travel—immersion, suspension, confusion, awe, and breakthrough. We are starved for spiritual nutrition, in part, because we consume things which have no calories and no nutritional value. It is for this reason that Byung-Chul Han goes so far as to call the "selfie" phenomenon not only addictive but pathological, a disease in which I have lost interest in everything but my own face. But precisely because I've lost the ability to be nourished by anything outside of me, the images leave me hungry, and so I keep consuming, and keep posting and posting. Han summarizes this bottomless pit:

> The addictive taking of selfies points toward the inner emptiness of the ego. The contemporary ego is very poor in stable forms of expressions with which it may identify, which would give it a solid identity…. And just this insecurity, this *anxiousness about oneself,* produces the addictive taking of selfies, produces a *self that is idling,* and never comes to rest. Faced with its inner empitness, the subject of the selfie tries in vain *to produce itself….* It is not a narcissistic self-love or vanity which generates the addictive taking of selfies, but an inner emptiness.[1]

If I'm right, then, we are losing the ability to be moved by still things because we are moving too fast to be quiet in front of them. We might have come to stand before these places of awe, moved by the noble desire to heal our own inner emptiness, but, standing in front of them, we don't know what to do, and so we start to fidget, spiritually. And in a desire to do *something,* we take pictures which we will recontextualize in a "fast-moving" platform, where they will make up part of our selfie narratives, the split-second content for other peoples' violent, late-night, sad-hearted, envious episodes of bottomless scrolling: here's *her* in front of the waterfall; now she's in front of a famous valley; here's *her* in Paris— "100% you." If I translate what I see into a series of posts through which you can accelerate, engaging in an act of bottomless scrolling, then you

---

1    Byung-Chul Han, *Saving Beauty,* trans. David Steuer (Cambridge: Polity Press, 2018), 12.

can *feel* their importance, but only at the price of depth and complexity. And I need a lot

them, because as I flatten out the images, I will need to string them together to replace the

original qualitative experience with quantitative amplification.

But what is more, when I post these images, the reality is that I have forgotten to

look at the thing itself. Instead, as I snap that picture, I am already, in my mind, looking

at how you will look at me: *I* am the sort of person who stands in front of so many things

worth looking at. In other words, the attention moves from the phenomenon of wonder

onto how I look in front of it, and, thus, the life-giving, nourishing encounter with beauty

I described above is perpetually deferred. Then, starved for beauty, I participate all the

more feverishly in the attempt to consume it. Unbeknownst to me, I am using what I

stand in front of merely to amplify the power of my image, rather than allowing what I

see to empower my interior life. I starve my inner heart, while consuming outer experi-

ences. The whole world becomes nothing but a series of changing backgrounds for my

face, experiences I purchase in order to enhance my social value in the currency of likes.

And, in this way, we're losing our landscapes.

---

But does this affect how we read our texts? If, as we said above, literature is akin to

being immersed within a landscape, what happens when you lose the lansdscape? Do you

lose the primal analog which operates as the secret paradigm for reading in the first place?

Is this the reason we have trouble with the stillness of premodern literature? Lewis seems

to have thought so. He once suggested that there is now "an invisible wall" that separates

us from our ancestors:

> The 'beauties' which they chiefly regarded in every composition were
>
> those which we either dislike or simply do not notice…. We must recon-

cile ourselves to the fact that of the praise and censure which we allot to [premodern] poets only the smallest part would have seemed relevant to those poets themselves.[2]

In other words, if they could hear the critical judgments that we pass in college classrooms and put in Cambridge Companions, they would be astonished by how much we had missed the point.

In particular, Lewis had in mind the many tropes and schemes of classical rhetoric. You'll remember that you can begin a series of sentences with the same phrase, as Churchill once did.[3] This is called *anaphora.* Or you could repeat the exact phrase in the middle of a sentence to create a doubling back: "Reason, your viceroy in me, me should defend"—this is *anadiplosis.* Depending on who's counting, there are between 200 to 300 of these things, all of which have ponderous Greek or Latin names: antithesis, paranomasia, asyndeton, polysyndeton, hysteron proteron, hyperbaton, etc. In the past, schoolboys spent most of their time not just learning these names but creating compositions that employed these techniques, and heaped them up on top of one another, not just in English but in various ancient languages. For us, piling up such tropes and schemes gives a feeling of artificiality. We wonder: why didn't our ancestors do something useful with their school time, like Calc II? Our ancestor's stylistic preferences have become for us as inexplicable as their taste in robes and curling wigs. Lewis comments:

---

2    C. S. Lewis, *English Literature in the Sixteenth Century Excluding Drama* (Oxford: Clarendon Press, 1954), 61.

3    For example, see Winston Churchill's famous address: "[W]e shall not flag or fail. We shall go on to the end, we shall fight in France, we shall fight on the seas and oceans, we shall fight with growing confidence and growing strength in the air, we shall defend our Island, whatever the cost may be, we shall fight on the beaches, we shall fight on the landing grounds, we shall fight in the fields and in the streets, we shall fight in the hills; we shall never surrender...."

We must picture them growing up from boyhood in a world of 'pret-

tie epanorthosis,' paranomasia, *isocolon,* and *similiter cadentia.* Nor were

these, like many subjects in a modern school, things dear to the mas-

ters but mocked or languidly regarded by the parents. Your father, your

grown-up brother, your admired elder schoolfellow, all loved rhetoric.

Therefore, you loved it too. You adored sweet Tully and were as con-

cerned about asyndeton and chiasmus as a modern schoolboy is about

county cricketers, or types of aeroplane.[4]

Lewis's reference to motorized "aeroplanes" is telling: we moderns like sentences

made up of machine-like simplicity. We prefer Hemingway to Milton. As Strunk and

White put it in a classic college-level book on writing: "Vigorous writing is concise. A

sentence should contain no unnecessary words, a paragraph no unnecessary sentences,

for the same reason that a drawing should have no unnecessary lines and a machine no

unnecessary parts."[5] In contrast, our ancestors preferred the sprawling, brachiating effect

of language, rhetorical figures radiating out like branches spiraling off and around the

trunk of a tree, in complicated, overlapping patterns. But because we prefer the ruthlessly

efficient, mechanistic interaction of gears, wheels, and axles, the ample effect of the

language of our ancestors seems strange to us.

In sum, Lewis was prescient: the more time we spent around our machines, the

more we absorbed their "logic," and the more we felt the need to self-engineer our

inwardness to better fit the efficient spaces in which we dwell. Mechanistic metaphors got

deeply within us, and our brains got so sped up that we couldn't even feel slow time, see

---

4   Lewis, *English Literature in the Sixteenth Century,* 61.

5   William Strunk and E. B. White, *Elements of Style* (London: Pearson, 1999), 8.

the vase, or appreciate the poetry or landscape, even when it was right in front of us.

—————————————————————

It is in this sense that I have used "apocalypse" in the preface of this book. In a previous century, we worried about a nuclear apocalypse in which the beauty of our world would be scorched by megatons of fiery heat (fears that have now returned). Many of our contemporaries now worry about an apocalypse caused by changes in climate. Politicians and academics are the managers of these conversations, of course, and in their little committees and subcommittees and review boards they establish guidelines and flowcharts and make recommendations. What they forgot—or perhaps never even knew—is *why* we should care.

But the poets do not forget the *why*. They understand that in any apocalyptic eventuality—in which qualitative, layered spaces are obliterated by quantitative powers of magnitude—what we would lose, by losing access to the natural world, is access to the language of the heart.

Take Richard Wilbur, for instance, who in 1965, wrote his "Advice to a Prophet." In this unforgettable poem, Wilbur gives advice to the would-be street prophet, who, very soon, like some wild-eyed and fur-robed Old Testament preacher come back to Ninevah, cries out, "Not proclaiming our fall but begging us / In God's name to have self-pity…."[6] Wilbur's advice, though, would have surprised the experts and generals and engineers on the committees and subcommittees. Do not—the poem's narrator advises the future prophet—employ those astronomical numbers written out in scientific notation to tell us how many megatons of explosive power will be released by how many bombs. Those numbers are too large for us to make sense of: "Spare us all word of the weapons, their

6     Richard Wilbur, "Advice to a Prophet," in *Advice to a Prophet and Other Poems* (New York: Harcourt Brace and World, 1961), v. 3–4.

force and range, / The long numbers that rocket the mind; / Our slow, unreckoning hearts will be left behind, / Unable to fear what is too strange."[7] But also, don't try to frighten everyone by talking about the elimination of the human species. The reality is that if we're not here, we won't care. What you need to do, instead, is make this appeal: speak "of the world's own change." In other words, imagine a world in which human beings do survive, but the natural world is torched (like Cormac McCarthy does in *The Road*). We *can* imagine a world that has become perfectly ugly, a world in which all white-tailed deer have slipped "into perfect shade, grown perfectly shy" (because they have been poisoned by radioactive waste); a world in which no larks trace out high trajectories above us (because no birds live on); and a world in which all jack-pine trees have lost their "knuckled grip" in rocky cliffs of shale because every stream has grown so hot that they boil like Homer's mythological Xanthus, set on fire by Hephaistos, and, thus, all trout are "stunned in a twinkling." It viscerally hurts to imagine such a world, so sad and ugly and lonely, but not for the reasons economists supply. It's not primarily that we would lose access to resources. That may be true. But what Wilbur says is this: if we lived in *that* world, and if we had lost access to all these natural phenomena, we would also have lost access to symbols for things we barely have words for, and yet need to talk about:

> What should we be without
> The dolphin's arc, the dove's return,
>
> These things in which we have seen ourselves and spoken?
> Ask us, prophet, how we shall call
> Our natures forth when that live tongue is all

> Dispelled, that glass obscured or broken
>
> In which we have said the rose of our love and the clean
> Horse of our courage…
>
> Ask us, ask us whether with the worldless rose
> Our hearts shall fail us; come demanding
> Whether there shall be lofty or long standing
> When the bronze annals of the oak-tree close.[8]

If you've never seen a jack pine, its roots dug into rocky soil, can you say "tenacity" and really feel it? Can you get at "steadfastness" and "stability" and "fortitude" without having touched an ancient oak? If you've never seen horses break free and fly across a long meadow at a gallop, can you feel "courage" when you use the word? If we lose access to our world, do we lose our ability to do anything more than participate in merely functional communication? Can anyone really get at that sense of giddy jubilation who hasn't been surprised by the unexpected appearance and disappearance of a sleek dolphin's back? Wilbur makes the case that we need those experiences of the world, because we want to touch those values of the heart that are hard to summon forth without the help of the sensuous, slow, still, layered, complicated, and richly dense metaphors drawn from the natural world. He's on Yeats's side.

---

8    Wilbur, v. 23–30, 33–36.

# EPILOGUE:

## FRANNY CONTRA NEW YORK

I want to remind you that I had positive things to say earlier in this book. But I also wanted to speak openly, so that we have a keen sense of urgency, a sense of urgency founded on the conviction that our world is starving to death even while over-consuming empty cultural calories—that we are undergoing a kind of apocalypse of the imagination. And so, for us, literature is not a pass-time. We are not readers because we "like" books. Of course, we might sometimes simply read for entertainment, as Eliot relaxed by reading detective novels and Lewis relaxed by reading sci-fi, and my high school daughter relaxes by picking up her siblings' middle-grade fantasy novels. But, inspired by the vision I have articulated here, when we read with a sense of urgency, we are not reading primarily for entertainment. Rather, we are engaged in a deep reading, in which we find our hearts quickened, our spirits moved, and our souls enlarged. Those who are haunted by Joy would never describe their pursuit of the eternal—in prayer, in liturgy, in love, in literature, in music, in painting—as "entertainment"; rather, we hunger to eat, what Dante called, "the bread of angels." And, yes, while we're at it, we might look a little "mad-eyed," as Wilbur put it, if we're found reading introductions to medieval literature on the beach in California. But so be it: we're reading to close the gap between the beauty *out there* and who I am *in here*. And when we have experiences like this, especially if we have them often, and we start to "get good" at them, then we will, of course, also enjoy our reading.

And so, yes, we're coming to our studies with a sense of urgency, in part because we are weak and fragile and distractible, and, in part, because so few people value what we know, what we have heard, and what we have felt to be of infinite moment. And we know, at the same time, how almost everything in our "data-culture"—our hyped-up culture of acceleration and force and vertically stretched functions—feels inimical to depth, to stillness, and to the secret longings of the heart.

But I began on a hopeful note, and I'd like to end on one, too.

Although our world of bustle might be inimical to depth and stillness, to down-loading as opposed to streaming (Amazon doesn't want you to be able to buy songs any more; you have to have a subscription service so that you're never off their platform), nevertheless, we know that old things are deep things, and that they are written on the human heart, and that, accordingly, they emerge, sometimes, when we least expect them. In the same decade as Wilbur's prophet and Lichtenstein's macho men and McCarthy's young Bobby Western, there was also Franny Glass, from J. D. Salinger's "Franny." Although Franny comes from the brilliant, deeply literary, and very disturbed Glass family, you wouldn't know that from "Franny," because she has spent her life learning how to wear the mask of the vapid, overly emotional co-ed. Her boyfriend is the strong, silent, ultra-masculine type. We have entered the archetypical imagination of Lichtenstein. Franny is up from her elite girls' school for the "Yale Game," and, at the beginning of the story, two dozen other young men are also waiting for their girls. They are going to wear the same clothes, race around in the same types of cars, drink too much, eat too much, and rush off to drink too much again. Everyone is doing what they are supposed to do. It's going to be really "fun."

And so, first, Lane and Franny have to go to the obligatory "Right Restaurant" and order the right Martinis. So far, so good. But the weekend soon takes a strange turn, because Franny is weirdly out of sorts. Women are not allowed to be critical. They're supposed to be bubbly and shallow and optimistic and, above all, find everything their boyfriends say archetypically profound. But today, Franny is having a hard time keeping up her part, at wearing her mask, and at one point, she snaps: "It's everybody, I mean. Everything everybody does is so—I don't know—not *wrong*, or even mean, or even stupid necessarily. But so tiny and meaningless and—sad-making."[1] Franny is "sick of everybody that wants to *get* somewhere, do something distinguished and all, be somebody interesting."[2] She's tired of the notifications and the pep and the hustle and bustle. Not long after this outbreak, a little green book falls out of her purse. She's embarrassed and she tries to put it back in her purse, which houses pills, tissues, cosmetics, mirrors, and brushes, but Lane insists on knowing what it is. And in a bumbling sort of way—she's practiced so long at being the emotionally frivolous female that her powers of description are weak— she tells him: "'It's something called *The Way of a Pilgrim.*' She watched Lane eat for a moment. 'I got it out of the library....'" Franny explains that within the book, the anonymous Russian pilgrim, upon hearing St. Paul's dictum to "pray without ceasing," comes to the conviction that he has never really prayed before. And so, he wanders throughout Russia until he finds a paternal and benevolent *staretz* to teach him the Jesus Prayer, which he begins to pray, thousands of times, every day. After his staretz's death, the pilgrim decides to seek out deep solitude, so that he might, he hopes, perfectly internalize the

1    J. D. Salinger, "Franny," in *Franny and Zooey* (Boston: Little, Brown and Company, 1961), 26.

2    Salinger, 30.

spirit of prayer. He doesn't want to not be present to Jesus any longer. And so, he goes off into the great forests of Siberia. During the day, he sits under trees and reads his *Philokalia*; during the night, he walks and prays in the cool of a northern summer.

Lane quickly loses interest in her explanation, and, at one point, impatiently asks: "I mean what *is* the result that's supposed to follow? All this synchronization business and mumbo-jumbo." Franny responds: "You get to see God. Something happens in some absolutely non-physical part of the heart…and you see God, that's all."[3]

We have found the source of Franny's unhappiness. Like the pilgrim, she longs for depth, for meaning—not for the trending, the up-to-date, or the fashionable. Franny feels trapped, trapped in her relationship, trapped in her world, and feels so overwhelmed by this suffocating sense of anxiety that she goes to the bathroom to weep in secret. Eventually, her fragile nerves are so stretched to the breaking point that she passes out in the dining room. She is carried to the manager's office and is, of course, a little embarrassed, but while everyone scuttles off to get water and phone the doctor, Franny is, at last, allowed to be at peace: "Alone, Franny lay quite still, looking at the ceiling. Her lips began to move, forming soundless words, and they continued to move."[4] Franny's trying to close the gap.

In conclusion, even in mid-century, modern Manhattan—the city of *Mad Men*; the destination of Wilbur's prophet, "mad-eyed from stating the obvious"; the city of Lichtenstein; the city of steel and glass and lights and marketing and Sinatra—in which everyone "wakes up in a city that never sleeps," in which everyone outruns their "little town blues," and, drunk on activity, "makes a brand new start of it" and tries to claw their way up, to become "king of the hill and top of the heap"—here, even here, the whispering voice makes itself heard.

---

3   Salinger, 39.

4   Salinger, 44.

And the old things feel much newer than the latest news.

If Franny could hear it, and want it so bad that she broke out into tears, then we can, too.

Our response to the whispering voice is the inner core of the literary life.

# BIBLIOGRAPHY

Auerbach, David. "How Facebook Has Flattened Human Communication." Medium. OneZero, August 28, 2018. https://onezero.medium.com/how-facebook-has-flattened-human-communication-c1525a15e9aa.

Barba-Kay, Anton. *A Web of Our Own Making: The Nature of Digital Formation.* Cambridge: Cambridge University Press, 2023.

Chan, Priscilla, and Mark Zuckerberg. "Letter to Max." Chan Zuckerberg Initiative, December 1, 2015. https://chanzuckerberg.com/about/letter-to-max/.

Churchill, Winston. "We Shall Fight on the Beaches." International Churchill Society. Accessed November 6, 2024. https://winstonchurchill.org/resources/speeches/1940-the-finest-hour/we-shall-fight-on-the-beaches/.

Coleridge, Samuel Taylor. *Anima Poetae: from the Unpublished Notebooks.* Edited by Ernest Hartley Coleridge. London: William Heinemann, 1895.

Davidson, Peter. *The Universal Baroque.* Manchester: Manchester University Press, 2007.

Eliot, George. *Middlemarch.* Kent: Wordsworth Classics, 2000.

Foucault, Michel. *Discipline and Punish: The Birth of the Prison.* Translated by Alan Sheridan. New York: Random House, 1995.

Hadot, Pierre. *The Veil of Isis: An Essay on the History of the Idea of Nature.* Translated by Michael Chase. Chicago: University of Chicago Press, 2008.

Han, Byung-Chul. *Saving Beauty.* Translated by David Steuer. Cambridge: Polity Press, 2018.

Hardy, Thomas. *Far from the Madding Crowd.* New York: Harper and Brothers, 1918. https://ia803108. us.archive.org/21/items/farfrommaddingcr0000hard/farfrommaddingcr0000hard.pdf.

Herbert, George. "Prayer (I)." Poetry Foundation. Accessed November 4, 2024. https://www.poetry-foundation.org/poems/44371/prayer-i.

Homer. *The Odyssey of Homer.* Translated by Richmond Lattimore. New York: Harper Perennial, 2007.

Joy, Bill. "Why the Future Doesn't Need Us." Wired, April 1, 2000. https://www.wired.com/2000/04/joy-2/.

Keats, John. "Ode on a Grecian Urn." 1819. Poetry Foundation. Accessed October 15, 2024. https://www.poetryfoundation.org/poems/44477/ode-on-a-grecian-urn.

Murray Krieger. "The Ekphrastic Principle and the Still Movement of Poetry; or Laokoön Revisited." In *The Play and Place of Criticism*, 105-128. Baltimore: Johns Hopkins University Press, 2019.

Lewis, C. S. "*De Descriptione Temporum.*" In *Selected Literary Essays*, 1-14. Edited by Walter Hooper, Cambridge: Cambridge University Press, 2019.

———*English Literature in the Sixteenth Century Excluding Drama.* Oxford: Clarendon Press, 1954.

———*Surprised By Joy.* New York: Harcourt Brace & Company, 1984.

———"Weight of Glory." In *Essay Collection and Other Short Pieces*, section 12. Edited by Lesley Walmsely, San Francisco: HarperSanFrancisco, 2000.

Marinetti, Filippo. "The Founding and Manifesto of Futurism." 1909. Italian Futurism. Accessed November 21, 2024. https://www.italianfuturism.org/manifestos/foundingmanifesto/.

McCarthy, Cormac. *The Passenger.* New York: Alfred A. Knopf, 2022.

Ovid. *Metamorphoses.* Translated by Anthony Kline. Ovid Collection, The University of Virginia Electronic Texts Center. Accessed November 17, 2024. https://ovid.lib.virginia.edu/trans/

Ovhome.htm.

Page, Kristen. *The Wonders of Creation: Learning Stewardship from Narnia and Middle Earth*. Lisle, Illinois: IVP Academic, 2022.

Salinger, J. D. *Franny and Zooey*. Boston: Little, Brown and Company, 1961.

Southwell, Robert. "Christ's Bloody Sweate." In *The Complete Poems of Robert Southwell, S.J.*, 137-138. Edited by Rev. Alexander B. Grosart. London: Robson and Sons, 1872. https://www.google. com/books/edition/The_Complete_Poems_of_Robert_Southwell/oNFTAAAAcAA-J?hl=en&gbpv=0.

Spenser, Edmund. "Epithalamion." Poetry Foundation. Accessed October 29, 2024. https://www. poetryfoundation.org/poems/45191/epithalamion-56d22497d00d4.

Strunk, William, and E. B. White. *The Elements of Style*. London: Pearson, 1999.

Verne, Jules. *Around the World in Eighty Days*. Translated by George M. Towle. Boston: James R. Osgood and Company, 1876.

Wilbur, Richard. "Advice to a Prophet." In *Advice to a Prophet and Other Poems*. New York: Harcourt Brace and World, 1961.

Yeats, W. B. "The Lake Isle of Innisfree." Poetry Foundation. Accessed November 15, 2024. https:// www.poetryfoundation.org/poems/43281/the-lake-isle-of-innisfree.

———"A Prayer for My Daughter." Academy of American Poets. Accessed November 15, 2024. https:// poets.org/poem/prayer-my-daughter.

Zuboff, Shoshana. *The Age of Surveillance Capitalism: The Fight for a Human Future at the New Frontier of Power*. New York: PublicAffairs, 2019.